Oh God
It Hurts!

A book about pain, suffering, and the 'love' of God

John Allen Thornton

DEDICATION

For anyone who has suffered pain and not understood it. May you find comfort.

CONTENTS

The contents of this book are my own opinions and ideas. In this book I will share my personal views on many issues. I will also share real life stories. The names have been changed and the details disguised a bit, so please do not think, 'I know who he is talking about" for you may well be wrong. If you do not like my views, or my opinions, or my perspectives, I am open to dialogue, if it is done in a polite and considerate way. You can email me at ohgodithurtsbook@gmail.com and I might reply.

ACKNOWLEDGMENTS

Cover art by Dedefox

1 AN INTRODUCTION

If this were a science fiction novel, I would begin with some exciting event which might foreshadow the main plot arc for the book. That would involve world building, introduction of characters, and a buildup or foundation for the adventure or conflict. I like well written science fiction. This book is not science fiction.

If this were a stuffy, dry, academic work, or textbook, there would be lots of footnotes and comparisons between various scholar's ideas. I would be forced to follow someone's 'Guide to Academic, Theses, Dissertations, and other Boring Stuff' or something like that. There would be a Table of Contents. There also might be a glossary of important terms, an appendix, a bibliography, and other things like that. I would be very limited in how often I was able to speak in first person which would restrict my expression and hinder my communication, and I would not like it at all. I would probably not be able to say stuff in common speech or address you directly. I would be forced to say things like, "In the opinion of this author, Scholar Smartypants builds upon, but differs from the core ideas which were expressed by Scholar Knowsalot, regarding the diverse matters which are, or have been, evidenced by...." Yuck. I have read way too many textbooks and other academic works. Frankly, I find them usually pretty boring and the way they are marketed to college kids is a big racket. They change a couple of paragraphs, and reformat the text a bit, just enough to mess-up the comparison of page to page from the last edition and mandate students buy the new edition for some excessive price. It is a shameful scam!

I am tempted to write this book in second person so you can choose your own adventure, but that would mean you would be jumping from page to page and that probably would not work, even though it sounds tempting. I would have to write a number of alternative endings and then index them and chop them up and make sure the pages all were accurate and the directions were precise and each storyline went where it was supposed to go, most ending in disaster of some form or another.

"You are standing before a small white cottage at the edge of a mysterious and dark forested area. A blue mailbox is to your right. The driveway to the cottage is to your left. What do you do? If you open the mailbox turn to page 6. If you head for the forest, turn to page 11. If you..." Well you get the idea, right.

However, this is not a sci-fi novel, nor an academic treatise, nor a lighthearted and fun reading experience. So I will begin with a question. Is the title of this book, "Oh God. It Hurts!" a prayer or is it cursing? Seriously.

What do you think?

Write down your answer somewhere so you can compare the one you have written now with the one you will have at the end of this book. Seriously, go write it down. I wonder how many of you actually just did that?

And the subtitle, "A book about, pain, suffering, and the 'love' of God" has love set in quotation marks. Why? What is that all about? Are those the written version of "air quotes" which people do with their fingers? Is it mocking? Is it irony? Is it jesting?

And love, well, just what does that mean? Is that about a person's love for God or God's love for a person? Or is it romantic love? Wow, there is an image, 'pain, suffering and romantic love'. That sounds like some really gray area to me. How do pain and love relate? Does being in pain and suffering appeal to you? I hope not. So is the subtitle about something else? Just what do I mean when I write 'love of God'?

As you will discover as you read this book, I like questions. No, let me elaborate, I love questions. I ask questions. I get asked questions. And I have often found myself in heaps of trouble for asking questions.

Way back when I was in elementary school at Crestridge I remember a time of questions. Now might be a time for you flip to the back of this book and read the "About the Author" section. I will wait on sharing this childhood story while you do so.

Imagine me whistling a tune here.

Now that you are back, let me continue. Back at Crestridge I was asking a classmate of mine a question. As was usually the case, solely because of my last name. Yes, I was stuck in the back of the room right behind all the kids whose last names started with all the letters down to and including the letter S. There were a lot of kids who had last names starting with S. So that made for a long line of kids in front of me, and with only a few kids with names T U V W X Y Z behind me. Seating by alphabetical order is a really dumb way to assign kids in a classroom, at least to me. I am sure Steve Barrenson and Jeff Aaronson would disagree. Had I been in a town with more Dutch people, the V section would have been much bigger, but, alas, Omaha in the 1960s at Crestridge did not have a bunch of the Van or Vander or VanDen type of names. By the way, in college I would always sit in the front of class. It was my spiteful rebellion against the curse of alphabetical order from grade school.

So there in the back of that classroom, I asked a question of a neighbor. I do not remember the question, but I do recall the teacher's response. She was angry. She cried out to me, "John Thornton, you come up here."

So I slowly got out of my seat and plodded to the front of the classroom.

Mrs. Teacher asked, "What have I told you about talking in class?"

I declined to answer.

Mrs. Teacher said, "Please share with the class what you were talking about."

I declined.

Thinking she had shamed my questioning impulses away, Mrs. Teacher sent me back to my seat. As soon as the lesson began, I asked my neighbor another question.

"John Thornton, since you like to talk so much, you come up here right now," Mrs. Teacher commanded.

Again I plodded up to the front. I expected to be scolded and asked to share again. But Mrs. Teacher had a new discipline style for me. She walked me over to the chalkboard and sat me on a stool. She took a piece of chalk and drew a rough stick figure on the board. A little white man on the dark green board.

"Since you like to talk so much, John Thornton, here is your newest friend. Talk to him all you want."

The look on Mrs. Teacher's face was one of utter victory.

I had other plans. I obeyed Mrs. Teacher. I turned my head and looked clearly at the little white chalk man.

"Hello, little man. My name is John. What is your name?"

The class giggled a bit. That was more than enough encouragement for me.

"Oh little man, you should not say that kind of thing about our teacher. She is not that mean."

More giggles came.

"And she is not that fat. Saying she is fat is wrong. Little man you should not say stuff like that about our teacher."

Mrs. Teacher exploded. Not literally like in some weird sci-fi universe, but figuratively she was angry. In modern parlance you could say she was really pissed off.

(Disclaimer inserted here. Now if you dislike my choice of the word "piss" forgive me. It is a Bible term from the King James Version. Check out Isaiah 36:12 and 2 Kings 18:27. More accurate and modern translations of the Bible, use the term urine, but urined-off is not a cultural idiom.)

Mrs. Teacher was red faced and angry, as I said she was, well, you get the idea. She grabbed my shoulder and spun me about. I fully expected to get slapped, especially in light of what my mother did to me frequently at home, but Mrs. Teacher did not give me a bloody nose, but rather just sent me back to my seat in the rear of the classroom. She then went on with her lesson. I went back to asking my questions which the neighbor kid did not answer anyway, and the little white chalk man stayed in the corner of the chalkboard. That is until Mrs. Teacher saw him there. She marched over and obliterated my newest best friend. It was the shortest friendship I ever had. The way she used that eraser you would think the black would come off the blackboard.

With all due respect to Mrs. Teacher, I was a pain to her. I could use another King James Version term about what part of her body I was a pain in, but I think you get the idea.

This leads us back to the subtitle of this book. It is a book about pain.

What kind of pain hurts the most?

Is it physical pain? I will address that a lot in this book.

Is it emotional pain like being divorced? Or betrayed? Or doing and saying things that hurt others? Well, I will address those issues in this book as well.

Is it job site pain, like having a snotty kid in your classroom? I will address that in this book.

Is it relational pain? Like the pain inflicted on you by family members? Ouch! That is a nasty area to be in pain. I will address that in this book.

5

Is it spiritual pain? Or pain done by religion? Are those the same thing? Or is religious pain different than spiritual pain? If it is, how is it different?

Is it the pain from having a difference of opinion? Perhaps it is a pain which comes from disagreeing on whether the words "piss" and "ass" can appear in a book that has God in the title? But if the title is swearing, maybe that does not matter? Hum?

In this book I will also discuss those people who prophet off of pain. That last sentence is not one of the typos you may find in this book. Typos are another kind of pain to an author. I mean it when I write that there are people who prophet (spelled that way) off of pain. Are you asking, "What does that mean?" Good! Read on and together you and I will find out, if I remember to write about it.

Or maybe pain comes from some group dynamic? Have you ever felt peer pressure? The pressure to conform and fit in? The people around you who demand that you hold the right and acceptable views according to some group? We all have those kinds of forces applied against us. Where is that more evident than in politics? There is an old adage which says "Do not discuss religion or politics" and therefore, I will discuss both in this book. Sometimes I am spiteful. What kind of pain does politics bring?

But pain and love and God are not the only things in the subtitle: "A book about pain, suffering, and the 'love' of God." Suffering is right there as well.

Suffering.

Now, if you are like me when you hear 'suffering' you may see in your mind's eye a cartoon cat named Sylvester spitting out the words, "sufferin' succotash," and a grin might pass your lips. Perhaps you happily recall the Looney Tunes gang on the TV. For me, the TV was often the babysitter, perhaps because I was such a rotten kid that real babysitters would not suffer through caring for me more than once.

Or maybe not, because when I was growing up, if you were old enough to sit in front of a TV there was never a need for a babysitter. By the way, the phrase "sufferin' succotash" is considered by some scholars as a minced oath. You know a phrase that was swearing, but was minced apart by altering the wording a bit.

You know about minced oaths, right? When someone says fricken and uses it just like the F-word, well, that is a minced oath. Or OMG instead of using God's name in vain, that is a minced oath. Some scholars claim that "sufferin' succotash" was an alteration of the phrase "suffering savior." Now if this was an academic textbook, edition number five, I would need a footnote and proper annotation for that comment. But this is not an academic paper or textbook, so there will be no footnotes. None. Zip. Nada. Nothing. One thing you can be assured of, one of the prime things I learned in seminary, is the truth and universal applicability of the idiom, "scholars are divided on that subject."

But back to the subtitle. Suffering. Suffering is real and takes many and myriad forms in people's lives. Suffering is universal.

Suffering is real, but how do we deal with it? Now there is an excellent question. Suffering is a word that has been really minced in our society. Sometimes you will hear, "That person talks so much and I just have to suffer through it all." However, is that really suffering? Is it genuine suffering to sit and listen to someone speak to you? At the time you may find it boring, or tedious, or redundant, but are you really and truly suffering? I doubt it.

Suffering is much deeper and more agonizing than just disliking what is happening. Suffering is a gut wrenching experience. Suffering is something you never want to experience again.

What do you think about suffering?

Even though I really dislike Tom Cruise's acting, it is wrong for me to say "I suffered through yet another crummy Tom Cruise movie." That is a misuse of the term suffering. By the way, saying "crummy

Tom Cruise movie" is sort of redundant, right?

If you choose to engage in some activity, would you ever choose to suffer? An immediate response might be, "Of course not" but is that an absolute? Are there things you would legitimately suffer over and actually choose to endure the suffering? If so, what are those things? Would it depend on the purpose of the suffering? Or would the reason for the suffering matter at all?

Pain can and does lead to suffering. But how do pain and suffering differ? I will discuss that in this book as well.

So this book is about hurts, pain, suffering, some kind of love thing, and God. Be it blasphemous or be it blessing, those are the things I will be rambling on about in this book. Does that sound good to you? What are your thoughts?

In a way, this book will be a discussion of the theodicy thing. Theodicy is a question. It is a really hard question. In a basic way it is about how can pain and suffering, things which we define as evil, exist, if there is a God who is loving, compassionate and capable of changing the circumstances?

Let me phrase the theodicy in a different way. Pretend you are a parent, maybe you already are, if so then you are all set. As a parent, would you let your child suffer if you could prevent it? What would your response be to your child who cried out, "Oh it hurts!"?

I will be discussing that question as well, and many others as we journey together through this book. I will share personal stories from my life, and I will try hard to relate them as accurately as possible. My sister Kay recently died (January 2015) and I am glad she and I could talk often in the last few years. We would call each other three or more times a week so we could compare notes, catch up on life events, and confirm memories of what happened to us as children. Talking to my sister reminds me that I better warn you again. My dad has been gone for decades, but he had a wide and earthy sense of humor and some of his stories will appear in these pages as well.

For example, previously I used the King James Version term, piss. Some of you may have already stopped reading because I said that. Alas, that is your choice. My dad had a saying, and maybe you had a dad like this as well. He said to me many times, "John it is better to be pissed-off than pissed-on." Yup, that was my dad's philosophy in a nutshell. So sometimes in this book there may be a raw figure of speech or idiom. You are warned.

As I said, I will share personal stories from my own life. I am the only surviving member of my family of origin, and I will try to be accurate and honest to what I remember. I now have no one I can call and ask, "Hey do you remember when?" I will alter some names to make them minced up, like calling that grade school teacher, Mrs. Teacher, partly because I do not remember the specific names, and also to protect the innocent, like Joe Friday always did. Throughout this book remember, my opinions and ideas are mine and as to the big issues, well, scholars are divided on the issues.

Oh God. It hurts!

2 PHYSICAL PAIN

In some very real ways, physical pain is the easiest kind of pain. It can be observed, sometimes. Physical pain can be treated, sometimes. Other people will acknowledge that physical pain is real, sometimes. We also have some control over physical pain in that our choices will affect what kinds of physical pain we endure. That is unless we are puppets on a string. Also, physical pain does protect us as a teaching tool.

Here is a life lesson. I once was moving a hide-a-bed. You remember those crazy couch-bed combinations, right. They were often hideously heavy and bulky. Well, once I was moving a big, ugly, heavy hide-a-bed by myself. I was a young, strong, and tough man. This happened long before I had artificial joints. While I was lifting that monstrosity the bed part started to fold open. I reached across and muscled it back, almost all the way closed. Unfortunately for me, the folding mechanism which extended the bed caught my arm in a really significant pinch. I looked down and saw the two metal struts were biting into me. Yuck. I had to then tip that hide-a-bed back so that the bed part folded open again, to release my arm. After doing that, I was able to set the thing down and fold it back together. The pain from that pinch taught me to never try to move a hide-a-bed ever again, especially alone. Lesson learned! All thanks to my friend physical pain. What lessons have physical pain taught you? Is physical pain a gift from a loving God?

When I was an Intensive Care Registered Nurse I would often ask my patients, "Please rate your pain with one being no pain at all and ten being the worst pain you can imagine."

You know, that scale for pain is really limited. Some tough-guy macho man would be sweating bullets and clutching and unclutching his fists and say, "Not too bad, maybe a three." I would then give him some IV morphine and he would only get partial relief. Another patient would tell me his pain was a nine but showed no signs of outward distress, and would sleep soundly after an oral analgesic. Pain is very subjective and cannot be compared from one person to another. Have you heard the old saying about the difference between major pain and minor pain? Any pain you have is minor, and any pain I have is major. Yes pain is subjective.

I have known physical pain very well in my own life. I have had eight joint replacements, starting over twenty years ago when I was thirty-two years old. More about that later.

Once when I was about six years old I was chasing my sister who was twelve. She ran out past the sliding glass door and pulled it shut behind her. Well I punched at her and put my hand through the glass. A shard of broken glass cut my right wrist just a small distance away from the artery. Youch!

Oh God. It hurts!

My sister was frightened and I was in pain. My wrist was bleeding all over the place, broken glass was scattered around the ruined sliding door, and neither of us knew what to do. We were just kids.

The phone rang. It was a neighbor lady named, Mrs. K. I have no idea why she called. Her son Ryan, my best friend for many years, was not at our house at the time. Somehow, for some reason, she telephoned at just that right moment. Coincidence? I think not.

Well Mrs. K heard the fear in my sister's voice, and she heard me yelling in the background. Neither of us cried, thanks in a large part to our mother's training of us. Tears were not allowed in our house. Being forbidden to cry is its own kind of pain which I will get to later. Well, Mrs. K came rushing over, she lived about two blocks away, and she took me to the hospital. Even though I asked numerous times over the years, I never did find out where my parents were on that fateful day. Kay did not know, and neither did I. My mom would just answer, "That was a long time ago and you should not have hit that window." Yes, blame the victim, just one of mom's many talents.

At the hospital they put stitches into my wrist and fixed the injury. I received my first four of over two-hundred stitches I would eventually have in my life. I probably have gotten more stitches since I wrote this. Shall we say two-hundred and counting? While the doctor was sewing me up, Mrs. K was there. I was lying on the table and she sat and just looked down at me. She had the kindest expression on her face. With tender and loving hands she gently stroked my hair. It was a beautiful act I have never forgotten. The most nurturing touch I ever received as a child, all from a neighbor lady who showed me compassion. Was that 'love of God'?

So that was an early experience of mine with physical pain. I have older and more painful childhood experiences with physical pain and I will get to those later.

What kinds of physical pains have you had? What were the causes of those pains? Was it from your own actions? Did it result from the actions of others? Was it just an accident? Did anyone come along side of you to assist? Who was a Mrs. K to you? Have you been a Mrs. K to someone else?

Mrs. K was not immune to pain herself. Some years later, her son Ryan, my childhood friend, died in a truck-train accident. Ryan and I had grown apart in junior high school. His family had sold their house and moved away. We still attended the same schools, but he was no longer part of the neighborhood group of kids. He was one year ahead of me in school and when the tenth graders, like Ryan, went to Burke and I was still in ninth grade, at Beveridge, well we just did not keep up our friendship. In high school Ryan was very much into sports like wrestling while I was very much into ROTC. Our paths did not cross much.

I recall vividly the last time I spoke with him. We crossed paths on the campus of the University of Nebraska at Omaha. We were both in college. I was walking to one class and he was heading a different way. We exchanged some pleasantries, he teased me about my getting married not long before that. With his wrestler skills he nudged my left hand with his toe. The new ring on my finger was there. I had not invited Ryan to the wedding, had not even thought about it. He was just an old friend from childhood. But that moment was special. Again, for just a short while we were two little boys connecting and sharing and pondering what the world was all about. During that brief encounter, I did wish I had kept in touch with him, but it had been eight years since we had been close friends, so I just gave him a smile and walked away. We went our separate ways, never knowing it was the last time we would ever speak. I graduated, moved out of state, and became a nurse, he stayed in Omaha and became a fireman, or so I was told.

About ten years later, Ryan died. No one even told me he had been killed until long after it had happened. I was told he had become a fireman and his truck struck a train. From the third-hand reports I got, he and his dog burned to death in the fire of his truck. Now that would have been excruciating physical pain. Why did that happen? Where was a loving God when one of his children was burning to death in a truck?

Oh God. It hurts!

And there was more than physical pain to that incident. I believe he had a wife and a couple young children. I wonder who was a Mrs. K to Ryan's mom in her extreme anguish and pain? Who held Ryan's widow when she faced horrid suffering? Who told Ryan's children that their athletic, energetic, devoted Christian father was never coming home to them again? Who would show them compassion and gentleness and mercy? Who would heal their pains?

Oh God. It hurts!

As an RN I saw physical pain in the lives of every patient I cared for. I was the kind of nurse who was willing to give pain killers liberally as long as it was legal and ethical to do so. I saw some nurses who would be stingy and miserly to patients regarding analgesics when the patient was in pain. Sadly, some patients did not receive the pain relievers they needed because certain nurses just did not like them. Yes, nurses are people and sometimes are petty. More often than that, I saw nurses who were too overworked because of inadequate staffing. This was especially true of the nurses in hospital wards. It is a truly hard job to properly tend to a large number of patients. How do you get the pain shot to the man in room 5 when the woman in room 12 just started vomiting? Those kinds of conflicts of time and calling wear on the emotions of nurses. When hospitals or nursing homes do not properly staff their floors with nurses, patient care suffers, pain increases, and people hurt.

But what is the origin of physical pain?

Way back in the beginning we see pain described. In Genesis 3:16 we read, "To the woman God said, "I will greatly increase your pangs in childbearing; in pain you shall bring forth children, yet your desire shall be for your husband, and he shall rule over you."

Time for some hard questions. God says to the woman that her pain will be greatly increased. This is directly referring to physical pain, the pain a woman has in childbirth. So why did God, personally, increase her pain? Was increasing pain an act done by a 'loving God'?

Also notice in this same verse, where the pain is increased, that seems to imply that there was pain present already. Can you increase something that does not exist? So was there pain in the Garden of Eden where everything was said to be good?

Is physical pain a part of the normal human condition? Or is pain a foreign enemy to be fought off with all vigor and energy? Why does God not remove all physical pain from our lives?

Well, the Apostle Paul talks about physical pain. In 2 Corinthians 12:7-8 we read, "Therefore, to keep me from being too elated, a thorn was given me in the flesh, a messenger of Satan to torment me, to keep me from being too elated. Three times I appealed to the Lord about this, that it would leave me."

Okay, now here the thorn in the flesh is called a messenger of Satan. Now that sounds more like the origin of pain, right? Satan gives us pain, right?

So, according to the Bible, God increases pain for women in childbirth, and a messenger of Satan brings a thorn in the flesh to Paul. Ouch! Pain from all sides.

And in the book of Job, there is the celestial deal brokering done between God and Satan over the man named Job. Job 1:1 "There was once a man in the land of Uz whose name was Job. That man was blameless and upright, one who feared God and turned away from evil."

Job was a good guy, and yet he ends up suffering some really nasty physical pain. All kinds of really yucky physical ailments are heaped upon Job and in the background, God and Satan are having some discussions about just how much suffering and pain Job should endure.

What? Honestly, Job is a good guy going about his life in a good way and living righteously. He does not know that Satan is scheming to try to hurt him. He does not know about the celestial meetings in heaven between God and Satan where Job's fate is discussed.

Then wham! Job gets hit with pain, suffering, and agony. For what reason? I am super uncomfortable with the idea of Satan and God dickering over how much Satan can inflict pain on Job (or anyone else). Why would God even consider such a deal? What would you do if someone came up to you and said, "I bet I can make your kid hate you, if you allow me to torture, traumatize, and abuse your kid. Do I have your permission?" Would you bargain with that person in any way?

I would not. I would be tempted to punch that guy in the face.

I feel like I must add again here that scholars are divided on the issue of whether or not there was pain before the fall in the Garden of Eden, and scholars are divided on the issue of what was Paul's thorn in the flesh, and scholars are divided on the origins of the suffering and pain of Job. Scholars are really divided on the celestial deals between God and Satan in the book of Job.

15

I however, do not really care what the scholars what to argue about. I want the pain to stop. I bet you would like your physical pain to stop too, right? Because when you are in physical pain, you probably are not wanting some kind of theological discussion, or blame, or an intellectual pondering on the noble character that pain can achieve. You want the pain to stop. Pretty simple, just stop the pain.

God has the power to stop all physical pain. But for some reason, that does not happen. Why is that, do you suppose? Is it because God does not like you? Does it feel like God is mad at you and is punishing you for some infraction? Is it because of some other reason? Is God just capricious and mean?

Satan does not want to stop physical pain because Satan is criminally insane and likes to hurt people. I sometimes think of Satan like The Joker on Batman. Not the comedic or silly and campy versions of The Joker like the one played by Cesar Julio Romero, Jr. in the 1960s, not that Joker. No, Satan is more like The Joker of the graphic novels who is truly criminally insane. At his core The Joker is a homicidal sadistic maniac with a warped and twisted sense of humor. He is a soulless serial killer whose plans make sense to no one but himself. Yes, The Joker, and Satan enjoy pain. They both enjoy killing, creating mayhem, and causing chaos. I wonder if the writer who created The Joker for the Batman series thought he was writing about a person who reflects Satan's characteristics?

Satan has the personality to perpetuate pain, and a huge book could be written about all the questions I have regarding Satan. Suffice it to say I do not think Satan will ever restrain himself from hurting people. Unless that restraint would result in even more pain and suffering later. And if Satan did offer you a way to alleviate pain, there would be a big catch. After all, Satan is jealous of God's creative power, and since creating chaos, pain and suffering is all Satan can create, he works diligently to do that.

Are Satan and God the only possible sources or causes of physical pain? Nope.

You are the cause of physical pain. Yes, you. No, not every pain is because of something you have personally done, but sometimes you are the specific cause of physical pain in your life. And you can cause physical pain to someone else.

Just like my choice to try to move a hide-a-bed, we all do stupid things that cause ourselves physical pain. There are tons of things we chose to do to ourselves that cause us physical pain. Poor diet, lack of exercise, bad sleep habits, foolish risks, and so many others.

For example, consider tobacco smoking. Yes, smoking is something a person chooses to do which will cause physical pain, suffering, and in the end agony and premature death.

Both my parents died prematurely because they smoked cigarettes. My father died of lung cancer in 1989. I was an ICU RN at the time and had been nagging my parents to quit smoking ever since I was a small child. I vividly remember a phone call I had once with my dad. It was about eight months before he died. Here is how that call went.

Dad: "Hi John I have quit smoking."

Me: "Why?"

Dad: "Because it is the right thing to do. You always say that."

Me: "Dad, why did you quit smoking?"

Dad: "Come on, be happy for me, I quit smoking."

Me: "Why?"

Dad: "I just did. Well, you see the other morning…."

Me: "What happened the other morning?"

Dad: "I coughed up some blood… just a bit."

Me: "How much blood did you cough up?"

Dad: "Well... A handful and it looked like a chunk of liver."

Me: "So dad, this is what you need to do now..."

I then worked with my dad to get to the doctor, but the lung cancer was spread all over his chest. Eight months later, two days before my thirtieth birthday, my dad died because he chose to smoke cigarettes. His burial was on my birthday. Happy birthday to me, I bury my dad. Those lyrics just do not sing very well.

My mom and sister watched him cough out his last months, and they still continued to smoke. My mom died of lung cancer in 2000 and smoked up to her dying day. My sister smoked until her last days when she died in 2015. My sister was 61, and smoking played a huge role in her death and caused her so much physical pain and suffering.

I am really tired of getting phone calls where I learn a friend of mine was diagnosed with lung cancer. Virtually every single one of those calls come from someone who smoked tobacco.

And consider what smoking does to the children around it. Children who see their parents smoking are witnessing a slow suicide. Yes, smoking is assisted suicide via tobacco. What kind of emotional pain is inflicted on a child who hears in school or on TV that smoking is a killer, and then watches his or her mom or dad smoke?

I tried so hard to get my parents and my sister to stop smoking, but the addiction was too hard, and the drug was too enticing, and the tobacco was too much to overcome.

Here is how one of those attempts went. I was about seven years old when I tried this.

Me: "Mom, why do you smoke? In school they say that smoking is really bad. If you quit you will live longer."

Mom: "Quit pestering me about smoking. I don't want to live

longer. That would mean more time seeing you."

Ouch! Her response was wrong in so many ways. At least that time she did not give me a bloody nose.

Smoking is just plain stupid. Here is a question, why is tobacco legal? Why is tobacco legal? I am cynical enough to say it is because of taxes and money and farmers who work for the tobacco drug lords. Tobacco is a proven killer. Why is tobacco legal?

What are you doing that will cause you physical pain? And what do those choices you make do to the people around you?

What do you do about physical pain that hits you out of the blue and has no rational cause or reason at all?

Where is a loving, compassionate, all powerful God in the midst of pain, suffering and physical ailments?

Oh God. It hurts!

3 EMOTONAL PAIN

I think Mrs. K's family knew something was not right in my family long before I put my fist into that sliding door window and she had to drive me to the hospital. Did I tell you how nice she was to me as they stitched up my wrist?

Well, Ryan and his family would invite me to go with them to church. They belonged to a Nazarene church and were active Christians. I tagged along because they were doing some fun stuff, and I wanted to spend time with my friend Ryan. Camp outs, picnics, shedding, and even Sunday School and Vacation Bible School were things Mrs. K brought me to along with her own children.

But going to church was not all I did with my childhood friend Ryan. We played together often. My neighborhood was a suburb. There was one lot which had an odd slope to it and no one had built a house on it. We called it the Vacant Lot, and it was a baseball diamond, a football field, an airport for model airplanes, a soccer field, a place to dig for lost treasurers, and everything else young minds could imagine.

On the lower side of the Vacant Lot, there was a grove of trees. Underneath it was all overgrown and there were rocks in among the itch weed, the spear weed, the nettles, and the other stuff we named because of what it did to us. One day, Ryan and I were picking up the loose rocks around that wilderness on the Vacant Lot. Ryan wanted to make smaller rocks that would be better for throwing, and I eagerly wanted to help him. So together we took a large flat rock and made it into an anvil. Then we took a medium sized rock and used it as a hammer. We put the other rocks on the anvil, and crushed them with the hammer. So there we were, two small boys smashing rocks onto the smaller ones and saving the throwing size ones that sheared off. What could go wrong?

I raised the hammer rock and it was getting pretty heavy by that point. Ryan was placing a rock to be smashed on the anvil. I brought the hammer rock down and it caught Ryan's hand. Ryan was a really strong and really tough kid, but he cried. She sprinted away to his house which was on a lot behind a hedge next to the Vacant Lot.

I stood there wondering what to do. Ryan was in physical pain that I had caused. I certainly had not intended to hurt my friend, but I had. My first instinct was to run away and hide. But then I looked all around at the trees, and weeds, and rocks. What had been a fun adventure-land now was a scary place as my friend was hurt. So I ran after Ryan to his house.

Mrs. K was holding Ryan in her arms in the bathroom running cold water over his hand. His tears were flowing and she was not mad at him, or telling him to stop crying. She did not use any of the words I would have heard at my house from one of my parents. She was just soothing his hand in cold water. She was letting him cry. It took me decades to understand why she was letting him cry. I really expected her to say something like, "Big boys don't cry" or the worse comment, "I will give you something to cry about." Those were what I expected to hear, but instead Mrs. K just spoke in a gentle and soft voice to her injured son.

And she even noticed I was standing there watching it all.

"Ryan, look, John is here. He is a true friend to you. He could have just run away, but he came to see how you are. That is a true friend," Mrs. K said.

Ryan did not glare at me or make some rude comment. He just leaned into his mother's loving side and let her tend to his bruised, but not broken hand. And Ryan never brought that incident up to me ever again. It was like they both forgave me. I wonder what would have happened and how I would be different if my own family had been like that regarding emotional pain. How different would Ryan have been had he had my mother? I wonder?

21

Comparing Mrs. K to my own mother is a study in contrasts. Sort of like comparing apples to hedgehogs. Let me share with you an experience so you can know. When I was a little guy, under six years old, for we were still living at the big house at the bottom of the hill just one house away from the vacant lot, I jumped off the dog house in the back yard. I was barefooted and discovered a nail in the yard. I found it by landing on it and it went way up into my foot. Oh my, did that hurt! I cried out, but no one heard. At least, no one came to my aid.

I tried to walk into the house, but every time I stepped down the nail went further up into my foot. I was just in too much pain and too little to think straight so I never thought to crawl to the house. Instead I walked up all the steps to the back door and called for mom.

My mom did come and she saw what had happened. She picked me up and took me to the couch. She grabbed a pair of pliers and just yanked the nail out of my foot. No words of compassion. No soothing and gentle voice. Just drop me on the couch and yank the nail out. I think she put on a Band-Aid and then left.

I knew not to cry. That just was not done in the house I grew up in. Did I tell you I often heard the phrase, "Stop crying or I will give you something to cry about"? That was not an empty threat.

So there I stayed. Alone and wounded. My foot hurt with physical pain, but the emotional pain was more intense. Just remembering that incident is unsettling.

Oh God. It hurts!

See the difference between Mrs. K and my mom? Yes, Mrs. K's family knew something about my own family that I was not aware of or understood. That is why they took me to their church with them. They knew that emotional pain is real, legitimate, and needs treatment.

But let me share a bit more about my mom. You will probably come to know her better throughout this book. When I went to nursing school in 1980, my mom, Anne, told me a story. My sister was living in Texas at that time, so she was not around home. My mom said she had once wanted to be a nurse. It was right at the start of World War II and she worked hard to save up the money for tuition. I believe it was $50. Anne then went to the nursing school and waited all night on the sidewalk so that she could be first to enroll in the new class of student nurses.

The next morning she was first in line when an instructor came out and made an announcement. The nursing school was closing because all the nursing instructors had been called up for duty in the war. Mom was crushed. She said it was a really hard time for her, to be all ready to start nursing school, and then have it dashed away.

What a heart rending story, right? Well, I thought so for a long time. Until much later when my sister and I reconnected. I shared that story with my sister and she gave me a funny look. She then said, "Mom told me that same story when I became a preschool teacher, except instead of being a nurse, she said it was a school for teachers."

My mom's story was just a big lie to manipulate her children. Yup, a big lie. There might be some small nugget of reality in that lie somewhere. My mom did live through World War II, but who knows what the real facts were? And her family of origin? I heard lots of stories about them, and I am convinced that her childhood would be well described as a nightmare. Her brothers and sisters were traumatized more than I can relate.

I believe family members might be the greatest cause of emotional pain. What do you think?

So emotional pain can often come from people who are close to us who do not treat us with respect, honor, or even simple and basic compassion.

Remember the subtitle of this book, "A book about pain, suffering, and the love of God"? So did emotional pain ever happen with people in the Bible? Did any of them suffer from emotional pain?

How about those heroes of the faith?

How about King David? He was a "man after God's own heart" (Acts 13:22) and yet he caused huge amounts of emotional pain. He also caused a bunch of physical pain when he cut off hundreds of men's foreskins (1 Samuel 18:27). The victims were enemies, and probably dead before the foreskin was removed, but still, that is a lot of slicing and dicing. For now I want to stick to the emotional pain this "man after God's own heart" caused.

You see there was a woman named Bathsheba. David was out on his roof and saw a beautiful woman bathing. Did David know where she was? Probably. Did Bathsheba know she was giving the king a show? Perhaps. One way or the other, David, was lusting after a nude woman. He then summoned her to his chambers, a king's command she could hardly resist, and they had sex. Now that I think about it, she could have refused, but she might have been banished or worse, but she did have a choice. (See what happened to Queen Vashti in Esther chapter 1).

Here is the cause of emotional pain. Bathsheba is married to Uriah one of David's brave warriors. The situation gets complicated when Bathsheba gets pregnant. So David tries a bunch of different things but ends up arranging for Uriah to be killed. David basically murders Uriah.

Now that is causing emotional pain. All over lust and sex.

David did not only have this problem with Bathsheba, but he also had encounters with other women, like Abigail, where his lust ran rampant and people suffered the emotional consequences. (See 1 Samuel chapter 25) Abigail is a married woman, and David wants her. He tried to get support for his gang of warriors from Abigail's husband, Nabal. He refuses. David then gets enraged and wants to kill Nabal and all his servants (1 Samuel 25:34). Abigail sends supplies to David behind her husband's back, and David is appeased.

To summarize a long and complicated story, Nabal (who is a mean and cruel drunk) ends up dying, and David gets Abigail as another wife. He had several wives, and all that relationship stuff was filled with emotional pain and suffering.

Oh God. It hurts!

So how does God look at a violent, lustful, adulterous, and murderous man as "someone after God's own heart"? That is a very good question.

How does emotional pain affect you? Is the cause of your emotional pain someone else's actions? Or is the emotional pain caused by your actions? Or is your emotional pain something from a situation you are in that no one seems to have caused? And what does God do about emotional pain?

Maybe King David is just an isolated example, right?

How about Father Abraham? When I attended Sunday School with Mrs. K's family I learned that church song about Father Abraham and his many sons. Do you know the one I mean? Abraham was called a friend of God. That is an impressive accomplishment, being a friend of God. (See James 2:23)

Abraham lies a lot. (See Genesis 12) In addition to lying about his wife, Abraham had sex with his wife Sarah's servant and knocked Hagar up. (At the time Abraham was called Abram, and Sarah his wife was called Sarai, but that gets too confusing, so I will just call them Abraham and Sarah) Oh, Sarah knew about the sex between Abraham and Hagar, she had even encouraged and arranged for that adultery. And poor Hagar, as a servant had no real say in the matter. She could have run away, but she was trapped as a foreign servant. Then when Hagar's son is born, his name is Ishmael, Sarah gets all upset and there is a huge amount of emotional pain in that family. Sarah and Abraham then have a kid of their own, Isaac, and that leads to Sarah and Abraham throwing Hagar and Ishmael out on their own. Yuck. Can you imagine the emotional pain that caused?

All that was done by Abraham the friend of God: adultery, lying, and betrayal. But it gets worse, and even more strange.

Friends are very important, right? Being someone's friend carries some responsibility and duty and obligation, right? Now I do not mean to sound cynical, but, would you ask your friend to kill his own son? Would you? Does a friend really ask another friend to murder is son?

How much emotional pain would that cause?

God comes and asks his friend Abraham to kill his own son. Yes he does. Genesis 22:2 "God said, 'Take your son, your only son Isaac, whom you love, and go to the land of Moriah, and sacrifice him there as a burnt offering on one of the mountains that I shall show you."

Despite what scholars say about that incident, I really do not like it at all. I have never found a satisfactory explanation for God ordering Abraham to commit murder. If someone asked me to kill one of my children, I would not think it was God, rather I would think it was The Joker or some other evil being.

So how do we understand the emotional suffering that comes from family dysfunction?

Sometimes it is almost too horrific to understand. Again looking to King David's family, we read about his daughter Tamar who is raped by her brother, Amnon. I guess you could say a half-brother, because they had different mothers, but they are all children of David. Well, another son of David, Absalom, finds out about the rape and waits for David to do something about it. David never does much. He apparently puts the value of his rapist son over the value of his daughter who has been raped. Real great dad there, huh? So Absalom implements a plan which kills Amnon and starts a rebellion. The whole nation is in turmoil and revolt because of family dysfunction. The rebellion results in Absalom's death.

And David knows emotional pain. 2Samuel 18:33 "King David was deeply moved, and went up to the chamber over the gate, and wept; and as he went, he said, 'O my son Absalom, my son, my son Absalom! Would I had died instead of you, O Absalom, my son, my son!'"

Oh God. It hurts!

So was your emotional pain to that extent? Or was it worse?

Mrs. K and her son Ryan took me to church where I learned some of the Bible stories, not the gruesome ones like I related above, more the flannel graph sanitized versions, and I was exposed to church people. I was allowed to ask questions, but I never did get all the answers I wanted. I think I pestered those people too, but they were nicer about it than some. No one made me talk to a chalk stick figure at that Nazarene church of Mrs. K.

So here are some questions to consider about emotional pain.

Have you caused the emotional pain?

I know I have done that, and not only to Mrs. Teacher when she tried to shame me into silence. There have been times when I was truly a mean jerk to people. There are so many words I wish I could take back, but once they are out, you can never "take it back" even if you sincerely regret saying something. I have emotionally hurt people.

Has your emotional pain been caused by someone else's crummy or worse behavior?

Long ago there was a public service campaign for something with a catch-phrase, "Words can hit as hard as a fist" or something to that effect. That always stayed with me, perhaps because my own family of origin had refined the hitting with words to an art form. No, that is too classy a way to put what my family of origin did. Classy does not describe my family of origin in any way. My family of origin liked to hurt people with their words and it was always a contest to see who could do the most damage to someone else with words as weapons. All done around the family events and the family functions. Holidays were a real joy, if you liked being insulted, wounded, and emotionally beat up. If one of their victims complained, they would say, "Where is your sense of humor?" or "It was just a joke!" or "Can't take a joke, huh?"

Tragically, the sins of the fathers and mothers are passed on to the next generations. Emotional scars are just as real, just as legitimate, just as painful, and just as long lasting as are physical scars. As I said before, in case you missed it, I have had over two-hundred stitches placed into my body, so I have lots of physical scars. Were I to count the "stitches" that hold together the emotional wounds I have had, I imagine it would far exceed the two-hundred plus physical stitches, stables, and sutures my body has had. How can you count the stitches in emotional scars? How do you even put stitches into an emotional wound? Who is there to be a Mrs. K and stroke your hair gently when the emotional pain is smacking you? How do you fix emotional pain?

Oh God. It hurts!

4 A SHORT STORY INTERLUDE

I love the Captain Kangaroo Show. That fabulous show for children was on from the 1950s to the early 1980s. That was all of my growing up years. Did you know there are no commercially available DVDs of the original Captain Kangaroo Show? There are a few VHS shows which are sort of like clip shows, and they are great, as far as they go. But compared to the thousands (literally) of shows that were filmed and broadcast, it is a genuine tragedy that the original Captain Kangaroo Show has faded into near oblivion.

I once did some research on a cast member of Captain Kangaroo for a different book I was writing. That book will not ever be published, due to the request of that cast member's family. During that research I found there are all kinds of odd things about why the Captain Kangaroo Show is not out on DVD. I could never get a clear answer on who owns the rights to the show. Scholars were divided on that issue. There was an attempt in the late 1990s to make an "All New Captain Kangaroo" which I have watched, and that is not too bad of a show. But as to the original, there may or may not even be copies of the show somewhere on 2 inch video tape. There are a few pirate copies of about a half dozen episodes which were made on Betamax or VHS and transferred to DVD. Some family members of the cast have a few VHS copies of a few shows. And there may be a couple episodes stored in a museum of TV and radio someplace. In my opinion, there may never be a release of any of the original Captain Kangaroo Shows, even if they do exist, because of various conflicts and trademarks, and whatnot. That is a real misfortune, our world needs more loving and compassionate TV shows for children.

Now why did I bring up Captain Kangaroo? Well to be honest, the last chapter started to get a bit intense, especially when I recalled my family of origin and emotional pain. So I mentally retreated to something from that era that was safe and gentle and loving. Yup, a character on TV. A man who spoke to me as if I had value. A man who wanted to gently interact with me and lovingly teach me about things in life: like animal, and manners, and being polite. A man who would read me stories. Neither of my parents were into reading to me. But there was TV, right!

Do you remember how much Captain Kangaroo loved to read stories? He would sit in his big chair, with his dark blue or red coat on. He would pull a book off the shelf and smile as he introduced it. He actually looked like he enjoyed reading it, and with his fine reading voice he would read me a book. In many ways, Captain Kangaroo was the best parent I ever had.

And so, here in the middle of this book called, "Oh God. It Hurts!" I am sharing a short story. Just imagine what Captain Kangaroo would think of reading this story. Perhaps it could be illustrated by some wonderful colored pictures and the camera could zoom in on those from over the Captain's shoulder as he read.

So sit back and be ready for a story about children, but not a story for children.

The Playroom by John Thornton

First written in May 2012 something like fifty years after it happened.

Scene One:

"I really have a playroom of my own? Really, mom?" Ten year old Katie asked. Her dark brown hair fell to her shoulders, and she smiled in anticipation.

"Yes, Katie, there is a playroom," mom replied. "And it will have all your toys, games, and everything. Right where you can always play with them."

"That's great!" Katie exclaimed and jumped up and down. She even grabbed onto her mother's dress, for a bit, in her excitement. "The new house is going to be so much fun. But I think I will miss my friends, like JoAnn." Katie was somewhat nervous about moving across town to the new big house her dad and his crews were building.

"Your friends can come and visit, anytime. And the playroom will have lots of space for you and your friends to play. There are two steps up from your bedroom, and there will be a door so you can shut it and play as long as you want. Your father has designed the house just as we want it," mom replied. She reached down and put her hand under Katie's chin and with a gentle upward touch made eye contact with her. "The playroom will be very fun for you."

"Oh boy, it sounds really nice. Will I be able to take all my things, even all the horses daddy has gotten me? Will there really be room?" Katie asked.

"Yes, Katie, there will be plenty of room. Your father is building quite the house," mom said. "His crews are working on it as we speak. Let's drive over and take a look."

"Well, JoAnn was coming over," Katie started to say.

"I am sure you want to see your playroom, don't you?" mom said.

"Yeah sure," Katie said.

"I will get your little brother. You get yourself ready," mom said and walked away.

Katie was unsure what exactly she needed to get ready, but she thought a lot about it. She decided she did not need a coat, it was warm outside. She did not need her galoshes as there was no rain. So she went to her old bedroom and looked around. It was perfectly neat and clean. The bed was perfectly made. The drawers were perfectly shut. The drapes were open in just the right way. None of the toys were out of place. And her eight horses were all lined up on her shelf just as they always were. Each horse was about a foot tall and made in fine detail. Katie's father bought her a horse figure, they were never called toys, each time they went together to a horse show. It was his way of making those shows special as their daddy and daughter time. There was the Arabian, and the palomino on the one end. And then came the paint, and the two quarter horses, her dad liked quarter horses best of all. Then the big black horse, and the white prancing horse, last of all, the princess horse. That was her favorite. The princess horse had a long flowing deep brown mane, and tail, with a beautiful body. The mane was the same color as Katie's hair, and that made that horse figure very special. Every looked just right.

"Well, are you coming?" mom said from the doorway.

"Yes, I'm coming," Katie said and hurried away.

They went out to the car, a 57 Packard Clipper Deluxe with a white over blue color scheme. It was six years old now, but ran very well. Their father always took good care of his cars.

"I like the blue best," Joel said. He was four years old and just learning his colors.

"You two climb in back, and shut the doors," mom said as she got in the front of the big car.

"I think the white is pretty too," Katie said as she let Joel in first, and then slid in on the back seat. She shut the door.

As they left the neighborhood, Katie saw her friend JoAnn and waved. JoAnn had been walking toward Katie's house. JoAnn waved back in a sad way.

"I am going to have a playroom at the new house," Katie said to Joel. "It will have room for all of my toys and games and even all my horse figures."

"Ma, what's a playroom? I want one," Joel said.

"The playroom is for Katie," mom said, as she turned the large steering wheel of the Packard, a cigarette held between her fingers. "But you will have your bedroom. The new house is very big. Your father is building it just right."

"I want a playroom!" Joel yelled.

"I will let you come and play in my playroom when you want to," Katie said. She was still thinking about JoAnn and wondering how JoAnn would ever come over to play. JoAnn's family only had one car, and her dad used that for work. Katie's parents were the only ones she knew who had two cars. Mom's Packard, and dad's 62 Dodge D100 pickup. Katie liked to learn the big names for the family's cars. She listened to what mom and dad said, and learned a lot about the family. She knew dad's Dodge pickup was used for work, and it had Benson Construction Company written on the side. That was her dad's company. She rode in the pickup when she and her dad went to the horse shows. She liked riding with her father.

As they pulled into the driveway of the new house, Katie was impressed with the size. The house was large.

Scene Two:

The new house was just about finished. So when they drove up, it all looked completed. Katie's and Joel's dad was just walking out from the garage.

"Dad!" Katie yelled and threw open the back door of the Packard before it had even stopped.

"Katherine!" mom yelled with some force. But Katie ran to her father and gave him a big hug.

"I see dad too," Joel said as he tried to climb down from the back seat. His mom had gotten the car stopped, and was walking over to Katie and her husband.

"The house is just about finished, Martha. I see you made it here," the husband said, with a good natured natural grin. It was too early in the day for his grin to be gin powered.

"Of course I did," mom replied. "Skip, are things done as we talked about?"

"Yes, the playroom is finished. I had to re-design how to access the attic, but the playroom will be right off Katie's room." The father, whose real name was Richard, but was nicknamed Skip was a good carpenter. He hugged Katie again, and then took a few steps toward Joel.

"Hey, how is the little turd today?" he said, and rubbed Joel's head. Joel looked very small compared to his father.

"What's a playroom?" Joel said.

Squatting down, his father replied, "Well, a playroom is a special thing for Katie. Your mother really wanted me to make it for her. When you are bigger you can have something special too. Come on, let me show it to you."

He turned and walked back into the garage with his children in tow. Martha followed. Her eyes were inspecting every inch of the new house. The brick veneer was very nice. The outside siding was painted a nice clear white, with black shutters. The neighborhood was new, and this was the only house on that new block with a three car garage.

They entered the house and proceeded up the stairs to where the bedrooms were. Joel was having trouble climbing the stairs, but was determined to see this mysterious playroom.

"Joel, come on and get up the stairs," mother commanded.

The dad stooped to pick up his son, but the mother put a restraining hand out and stopped him. Katie ran up the stairs quickly.

When they all reached the top floor, they stood in front of the bedrooms. "This is your room Joel," the dad said. He opened a door to a room painted in baby blue colors, with a new youth bed and chair. Joel ran into the room, and looked out the window. He was just tall enough to see out the front window. He could see mom's car, and dad's pickup in the driveway. "Your other stuff will be brought by the movers tomorrow."

"Wow, up high," Joel said as he studied the view from his window.

"Skip, I want to make sure the playroom is like we talked about," mom said and they left Joel in his room. Proceeding across the hall, they entered a room where Katie was sitting on the floor.

"It's so pink! Yuck. And all those white ruffles on the window drapes, I don't like it," Katie said. She looked at the big bed with all the frills and fancy pillows. There was a night stand with a pink shaded lamp, and a dressing table with matching chair. The room was like those in magazines, very feminine, and very idealistic. Everything matched, and everything was just as mother had wanted. "I don't like pink," Katie said again.

"Young lady, pink is the proper color for girls," mom said. "And those are the perfect curtains for in here." Dad gave his wife a glance but said nothing. "But come and look at the playroom," mother said in a more cheerful voice.

The bedroom was large and the window let in lots of light. At the end of the room was an odd angled corner with a white door. The door knob was bright shiny brass.

Mother opened the door, which swung out into the room and revealed two narrow steps. It was dark inside. Outside was the light switch which mother flipped up. The playroom lit up. The walls of the playroom were bright white, and there was a green carpet on the floor. The playroom was unusual shaped as the ceiling angled down the outside wall. There were no windows, but there was a fairly large space under the sloping ceiling. There was another door at the back of the playroom.

"What's that?" said the mom as she pointed at the second door.

"That is where the original steps led up to the attic. But I cut in an access way door in the master bedroom's second closet. So we can get to the attic that way instead. It uses those same steps. I just put a lock on this door," Skip turned that knob, and the attic door was clearly locked.

"Well, I wanted it sealed off, but that lock should work. Is the lock on the playroom door?" mom asked.

Dad looked down and answered, "Yes, just as you wanted it." Dad quietly walked out of the room.

Turning to Katie, who was still sitting on the floor of her bedroom glaring at the pink walls, mother said, "Katie, come and see your playroom!"

Katie walked over and looked in. She was amazed. There were already many things in the playroom. The walls were white, which to Katie was a vast improvement over the pink of her bedroom. There was a small end table next to the outside wall. On the end table was a small television set with rabbit ears. There was a table and chairs, and a bookshelf. On the bookshelf was a record player and speaker.

"This is for me? It is nice!" Katie was excited. She stepped up to the table and sat down.

"You can do all your homework in here," mother said.

"And I can put up my drawings on the walls, and stack things on the shelves." Katie began to imagine how she could enjoy the playroom.

"Yes, Katie, we will get your horses on these shelves, and you can have dolls and other girl's toys on the shelves. But you cannot put things on the walls. This is fresh paint, and we don't want to ruin that, right dear?" mom said.

"Okay," Katie said. She was looking at the record player and the television and was really excited about her playroom.

"Come along Katie, the movers will bring everything tomorrow," mom said.

They left the playroom.

Katie did not notice that the door to the playroom had the lock on the outside of the door. The light switch not only controlled the overhead light, but also the wall socket. It too was on the outside of the playroom. Mother carefully fingered that lock before she left.

When they went back down the stairs, they discovered that Joel had walked out onto the driveway. Dad was in the garage putting his tools away in his small tool box. Most of his other tools were kept in the large boxes which were bolted to the inside of the bed in the Dodge pickup.

"A big fishin' worm!" Joel said as he ran into the garage from the driveway.

No one paid him any attention.

Mother and Katie joined the dad in the garage. They were preparing to leave.

"A big fishin worm!" Joel said again.

"Katie, take Joel to the car," mother said.

"Okay. Come on Joel," Katie replied as she grabbed his hand and started for the Packard.

"No! A big fishin worm!" Joel said again.

"What's the little turd going on about now?" dad said to mom.

"Who knows, he just jabbers like that," mom replied, as she lit a cigarette. "The house seems okay, but you know what I expect..."

"Help! A snake!" Katie yelled.

Dad grabbed a shovel from against the wall and ran out to the driveway. Sure enough, a large bull snake had curled up in the sun on the warm concrete.

"For Pete's sake! Kill it Skip!" mom cried.

Skip chopped off the snake's head with the shovel. Then he scooped up the remains and walked around the back of the house.

"See? A fishin' worm!" Joel said.

"You hush up!" mom said to Joel, who backed away.

She then turned in anger and grabbed Katie by the arm, "What were you thinking? You can't take a baby near a snake!" Mom's normally brown eyes grew darker. Mom's eyes drilled into Katie's until Katie teared up and looked away. "That's better, but don't you cry." Mom shook Katie's arm once more and let go.

Dad returned from his task and said, "Well we had our first visitor to our new house. What'da think of that? I think I need a beer."

Scene Three:

Two days later, the whole family was back, and the house was ready to be occupied.

"Joel, you go play in your room, the movers put everything you need in there, and I set it up the way it needs to be," mom said, and dismissed Joel.

"Katie, your room is also ready. All your things are in your bedroom, and the horse toys are on the shelves in the playroom," mom said.

"They are figures," Katie replied. "Not toys."

"What did you say?" mom snapped in a low voice.

"Nothing," Katie said, and looked away.

"I thought so. Now go play in your room," mom dismissed Katie.

As Katie entered her room she saw that it was still pink on the walls, and still had the ruffly white drapes.

The playroom door was standing open so she entered into it. Her toys were on the shelves, and the horse figures were there as well. They were not in the right order, so Katie sat down and carefully rearranged them. She started with the Arabian, and then the palomino on the left end. And then came the paint, and the two quarter horses. She stopped and remembered the time when her dad had taken her to that horse show where he bought her the quarter horses. That was a great day. The horse show was so beautiful, and she and her dad had watched the horses, eaten popcorn, and he had bought her two horse figures that day. "Katie, you can have two, just like the two of us." He had then given her a big hug. That was back before Joel was born, but to Katie, it seemed like it was just yesterday.

She carefully set the quarter horses back on the shelf. They were nearly identical, but she knew one has a slightly different blaze on his nose, and the other has a bit more open eyes. Katie knew them by heart.

She then placed the big black horse, and the white prancing horse, last of all, the princess horse. She petted the long flowing deep brown mane, and tail, before she set the princess horse on the end where she could see it right away as she entered the playroom.

"You do like those toy horses, don't you?" mom said as she peered into the playroom.

Katie jumped with surprise. She had thought she was alone.

"Well, since those toy horses are so important, you make sure to take good care of them. It is your responsibility. Remember good little girls have good things," mom said. She then reached down and grasped Katie's chin in the palm of her hand. Pulling her face upward, mother said, "Do you understand me?"

Katie said nothing.

"Do you?" mom said as she squeezed Katie's face. Katie nodded. Mother let go, turned and walked away.

Katie sat in silence for a while. She held onto the princess horse and stroked the mane.

"Katie, I got a big boy bed!" Joel said as he ran into her room and up to the playroom door.

"You should knock before coming in," Katie said, but not in anger.

"Why?" Joel asked.

"Because this is my room and my stuff. So just knock on the door, and wait. Okay?" Katie explained.

"Okay, Katie. Wanna see my big boy bed?" Joel said.

"Sure, I'll come and see it," Katie carefully set the princess horse down before she left the playroom.

"Pretty horsey," Joel said.

"Yes, they are pretty. But you can't touch them," Katie said.

"Why?" Joel asked.

"Cause they are not toys, they are *figures*. They are only for me," Katie said. "Dad bought them for me."

"Okay, Katie. Come'in see my big boy bed," Joel turned around and ran back out of the room and across the hall.

Katie gently shut the playroom door, and for the first time noticed the lock on the outside of the door. It was higher than the doorknob, and was a sliding lock. The shiny brass of the slider on the door matched the slot on the frame where it connect to lock the door. Katie could reach that lock when she lifted her arm. But she did not want to touch it.

Scene four:

They had lived in the big house for about a month.

Katie came home from school, climbed the stairs, passed Joel playing on the floor in his room, and then walked into her bedroom. The playroom door was closed.

"Katie, you have about an hour to get yourself ready because your father will be coming home early to take us out to dinner," mother said from down the hall in her own master bedroom.

"Okay, mom," Katie called out.

She walked over and opened the playroom door. She turned on the light.

Tears welled up in her eyes.

The scene in front of her was totally unexpected.

She looked all around the playroom, and could hardly believe it.

Her horse figures were all over the floor. They were not on the shelves at all.

And they were broken.

The big black horse's legs were snapped off. The Arabian's legs were broken off as well.

Katie started looking at the broken parts, and tried to separate out the broken pieces. Not a single horse was intact. The legs for the quarter horses were scattered around, and she could not even tell which legs went with which quarter horse. And the princess horse was broken too.

"No!!!!" Katie cried out as she picked up the princess horse's legless body. "What happened to my horses?" Katie wailed in sorrow.

Joel came running into the room. "What's matter?" he asked as he turned the corner and saw Katie sitting on the floor of the playroom in tears.

"My horses are all broken!" Katie cried out. "Look at this." She held up the broken princess horse.

"Broken?" Joel asked in surprise.

"Katie, what are you fussing about, I need to get ready!" Mom entered the room and looked down at Katie.

"They are all broken!" Katie cried out to her mother.

"Well, you should take better care of your things. I guess Joel came in and played with your toys. You should have had them up on the shelves we built for you. I warned you to take care of your *toys*," mother said. "I guess this proves that good girls keep good things, doesn't it?"

"I no do it," Joel said.

"You go get in your room," mom said to Joel.

"I no do it! Horsey Katie's," Joel said.

"I said, go to your room," mom answered and slightly raised her left hand.

Joel hurried away.

"But mom, I did keep them on the shelves!" Katie cried to her mother. "I really did. They were never down on the floor." Katie had tears running down her face.

"Oh, grow up. Stop that crying," mom said, and bent down and harshly started to grab the broken horse parts and put them into a pile.

"But maybe dad can fix them? Or glue the legs back on, he got them for me." Katie was crying even more now as she watched her mom roughly pile the broken horses together.

"Come on, Katie, do you really want your father to know you cannot take care of his gifts? Really? He already thinks you are not responsible, and are a liar. You know your little brother obviously came in and trotted these horse toys around on the floor." Mom made a mocking pretend of playing with the figures. "Joel broke the legs off. He is just a baby and did not know any better. But you should have kept them on the shelves. I even had these made just to help you be responsible, but you could not even keep it cleaned up. I knew you would mess this up too."

"No, I did keep them on the shelves, I really did!" Katie was crying harder than ever. Through her tears she saw a horse's leg sticking out of mother's apron pocket. "There is one of the legs!" Katie pointed.

"Of course it is," mom said as she placed more parts into her pockets. "I am just gathering these up to throw them away."

"No! They are mine, you can't take them!" Katie was crying very loud now.

"Young lady, control yourself, right, now! Or I will give you a real reason to cry," mom said in a quiet and intense way. Her normally dark brown eyes were nearly black with severity. Almost no pupils showed at all. Her lips were thing red lines. She lifted a hand and her bright red nail polish was as stunning as the bite of her words.

Katie backed further into the playroom as mother gathered the last of the broken horses.

"But that leg was in your pocket before you picked up the others," Katie said, as she tried very hard to control her tears. "I saw it there."

"Nonsense. You are just imagining things. Again. You don't know what you are talking about. I have had enough of your foolishness. I will throw these broken toys away, since you obviously do not value your things," mom said as she straightened up.

"No, please!" Katie's tears were streaming out again. She reached out toward the apron to try to retrieve one of the horses. The head of the princess horse was sticking out of the pocket, just a few inches away.

Smack!

Mother swatted Katie's hand down. Mother then roughly pushed Katie back into the playroom. "Don't you ever reach at me again," mom said in a violent tone. "You have been a very bad girl, and you need to think about how bad you are." Mother slammed the playroom door shut. She bolted the door. She turned off the light switch.

"No! It is dark in here. Please no!" Katie fell to the dark floor of the now pitch black playroom and cried.

Now Katie knew why the lock was on the outside of the playroom door.

Scene five. The final scene:

Joel listened while mom talked meanly to Katie. She did that a lot. It really scared Joel. He stayed in his room until he heard the sound of mom's feet walking briskly down the stairs.

Joel quietly walked out to the wall by the stairs. He hid on the side, but peeked around. He could not see mom.

"Oh good, Skip. I am glad I caught you at work still," mom said

from somewhere downstairs. Now her voice was nice again. Joel
was confused. "We will not be able to go out to dinner..... Well it is
Katie yet again......No nothing is really wrong so much, it's just that,
well she is being a very difficult child again. You know she never
came out with instructions stamped on her butt." Mom laughed a
bit. ".......Oh no, no need for you to come home.....No I have it
under control. Just go out and get something to eat with the men. I
know you like Jumbo's Tavern.......Sure, Skip, have a few beers and
shoot some pool. I will take care of Katie and her antics......Just
remember, you work hard and deserve some time to blow off
steam........I have it all under control...."

Joel was uncertain what she was saying, and to who. It kind of
sounded like she was talking to dad, but he was not home. Joel
wondered if maybe he would come home in one of his good moods,
when he smelled like fruit, and talked all silly.

"Please turn on the light! I will be good. I promise not to be bad.
Please, please," Katie was crying.

Joel walked into Katie's room. She was not there.

"I am so scared. Please let me out. I'm sorry. I'll be a good girl,"
Katie was sobbing and knocking at the door from inside the
playroom.

"I help Katie," Joel said. He walked over to the playroom door. He
turned the bright brass knob and pulled. The door stayed shut.

"Joel, turn the light on," Katie said.

Joel flipped up the switch. The light came on inside the playroom.

Joel pulled at the knob again. The knob turned, but the door would
not open.

"Katie, come out!" Joel said.

"I can't, the door is locked," Katie said. She had a few less tears now.

"I open it,' Joel said, and again he turned the knob and pulled. The door would not open. He grabbed the knob with both hands and hung on it. But still the door did not open.

"Katie, you come out," Joel said.

"The door's locked. I can't get out," Katie said yet again.

"Locked?" Joel looked up. The bright brass knob was there, but up higher was something else the same color as the knob. "Lock on door?" he asked.

"Yes, the door's locked. Just go back to your room Joel. Don't let mom see you in there," Katie felt a bit safer with the light back on, but the playroom seemed much smaller now.

"I fix," Joel said. He walked over and grabbed the chair from by Katie's dressing table. He dragged it toward the playroom door. It dropped over with a thud. Joel set it back up and dragged it some more. Reaching the playroom door, Joel pushed the chair up against it.

"I fix the lock," Joel said. He climbed up onto the chair. By standing on his tip toes he could just reach the brass lock. He fumbled at it with his fingers. "Lock no turn," he said.

"What are you doing!" mom said as she marched into the room.

"I help Katie," Joel said as he glanced at mom and then resumed fumbling with the lock.

"Oh no you don't" mom said, and pulled him off the chair by one arm. She set him down hard on the floor. She snapped the light switch back down, so it was again dark as a tomb in the playroom. She picked up the chair and set it correctly down in front of the dressing table.

"You let her out!" Joel said, as he regained his feet by pushing himself up by his arms.

Mom's eyes grew fierce. She raised her left hand up to her right shoulder and swung downward in a wicked backhand across Joel's face. Joel's little body was knocked flat onto his back. His head thumped into the deep pile carpeting.

"Now what did you say?" mom said as she readjusted her large ring on her finger. She looked carefully at the ring to make sure it was in proper alignment on her hand. She then straightened her fingers out to examine them. She smiled a bit when she realized that her fingernail polish was not altered.

Joel wiped his bleeding nose with his hand. Then he sat up. Blood was oozing down from his nose onto his stinging face. He saw drops of blood spilling onto his little white shirt. The blood was darker colored than the fancy bright red color on his shirt.

"Oh no. Don't you get blood on your good shirt!" mom said when she finally looked at him.

Joel grabbed his nose with both hands and tried to push the blood back in to his nose. But it oozed out around his fingers.

"Get in the bathroom, now! And do not get blood on this new carpet," mother commanded as she grabbed Joel and nearly dragged him out of Katie's bedroom. She pushed him into the bathroom, and handed him a rag from the rag-bag under the sink. "Do not use the wash clothes or the towels. Now get yourself cleaned up," mom said as she roughly yanked the white shirt with the red colored collar off over Joel's head. She slammed the door shut as she left and was saying, "Well, a little club soda will take these spots out, if I get to it quick enough. I sure hope he didn't ruin another nice thing."

And it took Katie and Joel forty five years before they could begin to face all the memories they had of the playroom.

The End

What did you think of my story?

I must confess when I first wrote it, I was unclear of all that has happened. I sent it to my sister who is (I guess now I have to say was) six years older than me. As I said she died just ten days ago. After I sent her "The Playroom" she called me and we had a long, long talk about it. Yes, John and Kay talked about Joel and Katie. We talked about broken toy horses, and about a playroom that had a lock on the outside of the door, with a light switch you could only use from the outside.

Kay confirmed what I wrote. For her entire life, my sister had what she called "confinement issues" which wrecked her life in so many ways. Too many people dismissed it as "she is just a nut" or "she is making stuff up" or "it is all just an excuse." We also started to openly talk about our mom, who we renamed, mommatroll. Is that a violation of the command, "honor your father and your mother"? I wonder?

What do you think?

I am so thankful that Kay and I talked about that stuff and she had me to confirm for her that she real did endure that pain and suffering.

Oh God. It Hurts!

5 FAMILY PAIN

Do you get an idea where this chapter might be going? Well, yes I will be sharing some more fun and fascinating stories from the wonders of my childhood. Yee-haw!

First, let me say my mom and dad always provided well for my physical needs like food, clothing, and shelter. In fact, monetarily my dad made pretty good money as a contractor, carpenter, realtor, and homebuilder. From the outside, my childhood life may have looked blessed, or even privileged.

However, that was not the case. Money, food, shelter, and stuff does not a home make. A home must be a safe place to be a genuine home. A place that is not safe physically or emotionally is not really a home, it might be more of a prison cell.

Family pain can be just plain ugly.

My family had a code of silence. Even right now as I type this, when all the big and powerful people from my childhood are dead and gone, I still feel some dread and fear sharing these stories with others. But I am determined to do this. No child should be crushed by a code of silence which just covers over sin.

In a way, it is like when Noah was drunk and passed out naked in his tent. Yes, the biblical hero Noah, got drunk, and passed out naked in his tent. Did you know that was in the Bible? Well take a moment and read Genesis 9:18-29.

I will whistle while you read that passage.

So what did you think of that part of Noah's story? It is seldom made into a cartoon for children. Nor is drunken Noah part of the play-sets that have an ark with ceiling hole for the cute giraffe, and lots of animals along with action figures of Noah, his wife (her name was not probably Joan, by the way), his sons and their wives. Indeed, I have yet to see a Noah and the Ark playset that includes the tent and bottle of wine.

Just in case you did not read the Bible passage, let me recapitulate it here. Noah the great and faithful man is passed out drunk and naked. He has three sons, Ham, Shem, and Japheth. In the story of drunken Noah, Ham finds him drunk and tells his brothers about their father's drunken nakedness. Ham breaks the code of silence. Shem and Japheth make a big production out of backing into the tent and covering over the naked, drunken sailor Noah. Those two boys want to impose the code of silence and hide the drunk.

When Noah wakes up he is hungover and begins cursing and swearing. Now there are some weird people who claim Noah's drunken swearing is from God, but really? Come on! I seriously doubt God used a drunk in his hangover to deliver a message. What the Bible says about drunkenness is summed up in Proverbs 23:29-33 "Who has woe? Who has sorrow? Who has strife? Who has complaining? Who has wounds without cause? Who has redness of eyes? Those who linger late over wine, those who keep trying mixed wines. Do not look at wine when it is red, when it sparkles in the cup and goes down smoothly. At the last it bites like a serpent, and stings like an adder. Your eyes will see strange things, and your mind utter perverse things."

Drunken, and hungover Noah utters perverse things, and attacked his family.

The Bible does not say, "God instructed Noah" at that point. Nothing like that at all. It all is from Noah's alcohol infused mind. Noah does use the name of the Lord in vain to curse, but cursing like that is really common, right? So who does Noah attack in his drunken or hungover tirade? Canaan. Noah does not go after the man, his son Ham, who found him drunk and told his brothers. Instead, the drunken and hungover Noah attacks Ham's son. How awful is that?

All for breaking the code of silence about naked drunkenness. It sounds familiar to me.

Do you have pain from family incidents? Ham and Canaan sure did. They ran away from the drunk Noah.

Oh God. It hurts!

The code of silence was imposed on people in my family by "those in power." Let me tell you about some times I remember encountering the code of silence, and the facial looks that were associated with it.

Did your family have facial looks? Did you get, 'the look' and you knew something was coming? Did that alert you to the fact that family pain was coming?

The river ran pretty fast nearby as my cousin Mort (not his real name, but he was my real cousin and the stories are real) and I sat and talked. We were about ten years old. The sides of the bank had been a place where people had dropped old car bodies. Those were fun to explore. Some of them were part in the river, but most of them were just sideways or end ways on the bank. They were all really old and most did not have seats or anything like that. One did have an old back seat so that was where we went.

Sitting in that old back seat Mort and I talked. Mort liked to tell stories. I was never sure if he was making it up or what. He even said he liked to go around at night and look in the windows of the other vacation cabins. He was like that.

Well, I made up a song and sang it for Mort. I know now that it was based very loosely off the Caisson Song or the song known as "The Army Goes Rolling Along" with its myriad of various lyrics. I like to make up silly songs. Just ask my own children. They will confirm for you that I like to make up ditties and minced songs and jiggles. My one daughter told me some years ago, "Dad, growing up with you is like living in an odd musical." My singing has never been very good, but I can rhyme words pretty well.

So I replaced a bunch of the words for that song and put Mort's parent's names it in, along with other family members. In my own way, I made it a minced oath.

The chorus for my new song was:

"So we will drink, drink, drink, till we vomit, in the sink. We'll shout the order loud and clear. More beer!"

Perhaps I had heard that part in school, and it is not my original creation, but fitting it into my minced up song with the names of the family members was pretty funny. Or so I thought at the time.

As I finished my solo for Mort, which included some really nasty words I had heard from my dad. I also used some phrases I did not understand, but I used them anyway because they sounded grown-up. Mort just stared.

"So what do you think?" I honestly expected Mort to laugh. The words all kind of rhymed and I used big grown up works like our parents used. Mort was hurt, scared, and gave me a look. He got up to leave. Then I remembered another time I had seen Mort look like that. I call it the terror look.

As Mort climbed out of that old car body, I could clearly remember a time at our aunt's house. The oldest sibling of my mom, Aunt Agnes looked a lot like my mom, but older. She did not have kids. She used to live with my grandma, who I called her grandma, but Mom called her Minnie. That always seemed kind of odd, since my dad had a sister named Minnie as well, so I just called her grandma. (I only learned as an adult that this lady was my mom's step mom)

Anyway, it was at Aunt Aggie's little old house, a couple years before, that I remembered Mort having the terror look. We had been sitting in Aunt Aggie's front yard, by the steps to her house. We were eating cake. I do not remember why we were eating cake, but we were. Mort and I were trying to say words that the other one did not know. Soon we were saying big grown-up words. My dad had a wide variety of words, and those kinds of words are not in the King James Version. Mort gave me a sly look and went inside. It was not the look I saw after singing my little sing for him, it was a look of "I got something on you." That is a different look which I came to understand later. I called that look a term that ends with "___ eating grin."

Mort went in and told everyone what words I had been saying outside.

My mom came outside and slapped me hard. Some of my oldest memories are of bloody noses given to me by my mother. Yup, she hauled off and slapped me, then just turned around and went into the house.

Mort came back with another piece of cake. He was grinning from ear to ear and was very happy that I was getting slapped. He had that other look on and was pleased with himself. That happy look only lasted for a few moments. Before the bright red mark could fade from my face, Mort had a different look on his face. He saw the porch door open. The terror look came over him.

Mort's mom staggered out. That was when I saw the terror look on Mort's face. Mort's mom was drunk. I can honestly say that I do not ever remember seeing her sober. Mort was horrified and fell down crying, "Not me it was just John. I didn't say nothing!"

I felt really sorry for Mort, for he was truly afraid.

The terror look was on his face.

Mort was afraid like that as he climbed out of that old car body. I climbed out as well and tried to talk to him. I thought I knew what he had in mind.

"Hey Mort. What are you going to do? Run away like a little baby and tell your mommy?"

"You shut up. I'll do what I want." Mort was mad and hurt. He was about to run away. "Just don't ever, ever talk about the drinking. We can never talk about that stuff." Mort said it in almost a whisper and said it with immense fear. For a moment we both knew we were up against the code of silence. Two little boys against the family pain. Two kids against the giants and their hidden agenda.

Oh God. It hurts!

So did your family have a code of silence?

I mentioned my mom and how she slapped me. Well, slapping is probably not a strong enough word. It was not a closed fist, but it was powerful.

Perhaps my very oldest memory is from when I was wearing a white shirt which had a red collar. Sort of like Joel, in my story, I guess. I recall my mom grabbing me by my arm and yanking me up while slapping me. My nose bled. I can see in my memory, the blood dripping out and onto that clean white shirt. I see the trail the blood left as it ran down the front while other drops fell as I squirmed and tried to get away. I kicked my feet which were in little white shoes, but I was off the floor. Blood running down my nose, across my white shirt and plopping onto the floor. Fear and pain seared that image into my brain.

There were lots of times like that.

Another time I can remember my mom striking me, was at a funeral. Funerals were never a good experience in my family. It was the funeral for her step mom, whom most of the family called, Minnie, but I called grandma. I was about ten years old.

I was amazed at all the food at the dinner afterward. So, I was talking to Mort and had asked him about how much it must all cost. Did I tell you I like to ask questions? My mom heard me say that to Mort. I wish she had not heard that. I was in trouble. She took me to the side and pushed me into a small coat room. She said, "So you want to know how much a funeral costs?"

I nodded my head. That was a mistake. Mom slapped me so hard I hit my head on the rack of coats. She then slapped me back the other way, and then slapped the first way again. Both side of my face were stinging and my head was throbbing from hitting the rack. Mom then said in a lower and controlled voice, "Any more questions?"

I shook my head no. I knew not to say a word again.

Later, Mort and I were sitting quietly at a table and eating some nuts and drinking punch. We had not spoken about money since Mom had given me her answer. That is when Mort's mom walked up. She tripped over the end of the table. She caught herself by grabbing Mort's chair. As she straightened up she said to Mort, "Have you been asking about money?"

"John is doing that. I never said a word. Not a word. Not a word." Mort trembled and cried really hard. Again he had the terror look. She had not touched him, yet he cried as if he had already been smacked.

She grabbed Mort's face and squeezed really hard. His lips went together and even more tears flowed down his face. She raised her other hand as if she was going to slap him.

"You better not, you little runt," she added some grown-up words which no doubt were swearing. After a bit, she let go of his face. Mort fell to the floor and covered his head with his hands. He fully expected blows to rain down upon him. Had his mother not been so drunk, I am pretty sure the beating would have taken place right there in the mortuary. Instead, she nearly tripped again and then staggered away.

As to meanness, Mort's mom was bad, but I fear his dad was worse. My mom and Mort's dad were siblings and they learned their parenting style from the same source. As an adult myself, I can only imagine how bad they had it as children to turn out like they did. That does not in any way excuse it, but family pain is passed from one generation to the next unless extraordinary measures are taken.

Family pain can show up in all kinds of situations. It may be just in daily life that family pain happens. Or it might come from those special 'family times' when the family gets together for some event. I remember a couple of weddings which I attended as a child, one where I was a ring bearer, and another where I was an usher. Those happy events went off without incidents. At least to me there were not incidents of family pain. But funerals, now they are a different matter.

Again, my cousin Mort and I were together at the aftermath of a funeral. I was fifteen. The funeral was for another one of my mom's brothers. Mort and I were at the tail end of the group of cousins. There were not that many anyway, but we were the younger ones. So we were in my own backyard and sitting on the swings. If we stayed away from the big powerful people, it was safer, somewhat.

Mort and I both heard a commotion and so we ran around to the side yard where the driveway led to the garage. There we witnessed an event that is forever etched into my mind. It was the worst fist fighting and hand to hand combat I have ever seen.

It was between two of my older cousins. They were about eight years older than me, and they were literally trying to kill each other. Fists were flying and kicks were being made, and one brother grabbed the other and threw him to the concrete. The one on the ground pulled the other brother down and they were a tangle of flailing appendages. Arms swung with as much punching force as I have ever seen. Chuck Norris, Bruce Lee, and Mohammed Ali never hit anyone harder or tried more violently to injure someone. Those two brother were really fighting.

After a few moments of that, the adults in the house rushed out, those who were not too drunk to walk, and pulled the brothers apart, but they were still fighting and yelling and swearing and biting with their teeth at each other.

Oh God. It hurts!

And what was the melee about? Mort and I overheard that it was all about the dead man's shotgun. One of the brothers had taken the shotgun a few days before, and claimed it was because he was afraid his dad would commit suicide with it. The other brother claimed his brother just wanted the gun and stole it before the will was read. Yuck!

I have spoken in this section a lot about my cousin Mort. So let me tell you what happened with him. For alcohol did not just make people stupid at funerals, or make them mean at social gatherings, or make them kill off their livers. There are other ways alcohol can kill.

My cousin Mort loved the show "The Dukes of Hazzard." In many ways I think Mort thought that was a reality TV show and that was how you could drive and live.

In January 1981, Mort and I were driving along on a rural stretch of Nebraska highway. I had gone out to see him because he was having his twenty-first birthday. It was cold, frozen, and we were out for fun. Just driving around. Mort was driving his nice pickup that his dad had purchased for him. We came upon a railroad bridge. Now this was a rural one and it was wooden and shaped like an arch. The road led right to it and it went up and over the railroad. You could not see the other side of the road. But you could see the sign that read, "Caution Bump" as we approached.

Mort hollered out, "I like bumps!" with his best impression of Bo or Luke Duke. And he put his foot to the accelerator.

Now do not get me wrong, neither of us were drinking at all that day. I was attending nursing school but was off for break, and Mort had been working some odd jobs. It was morning, and besides, I never was much of an alcohol drinker. So booze played no role that day on a frozen Nebraska highway.

The pickup rushed toward that bridge, and when we hit it, there was indeed a great bump. At the top of that bridge, we were flying like General Lee. Literally we were airborne.

On the other side of that bridge the arch went down and the road made a really sharp turn to the right. The road was also covered in ice. We flew over that section of the bridge and landed the truck on that ice covered roadway. There was no way at all to make the turn, and we buried that truck door-deep in snow in the ditch.

Neither of us were hurt. But the truck was buried. We had to open the windows to get out. Do you know how cold a Nebraska winter can be? Especially when you are trying to dig a truck out of a ditch filled with snow?

We could not get the truck free no matter what we did. And so we looked around and then we walked to a farmer's house. We pleaded with him to dig us out. He demanded $20. Mort had no money, so I paid the farmer. He then drove his tractor out, making us walk alongside in the bitter cold. That farmer used his front end loader to dig out the snow, and hooked chains to the truck and pulled it out.

We got free from that snow bank.

Driving home I told Mort, "You owe me $20."

"You know that .22 revolver of mine?" Mort asked.

"Yes."

"You keep it and we call it even," Mort said.

"Ok," I answered.

About eight months later, Mort drove out to see a friend of his at a bar. He apparently got in that friend's car in the back seat. The friend was very drunk and smashed the car into the back of a semi-truck at a high rate of speed.

There were no slapping incidents at Mort's closed-casket funeral.

Oh God. It hurts!

Emotional pain is also a significant part of family pain. A real and good family loves, encourages, and supports the members of the family. Now, no family is perfect. For example, Adam and Eve lived in the Garden of Eden and walked and talked with God. That is a pretty good "growing up" and yet when they had kids, Cain murdered his brother Abel. That had to cause immense emotional pain for Adam and Eve and later for the other children they had.

So what kinds of emotional pains were in your family?

As I said, I think Mrs. K recognized the junk in my family and she and her family tried to help out. They took me to church, and camp outs, and lots of fun things.

One of those fun things was a church kids' sledding trip to a local park. The park had large hills and a lake at the bottom of the hills. Late one afternoon, we all piled into a station wagon and headed out with the sleds tied to the roof. When we got to the park, Jim, the youth leader, untied the sleds. Ryan grabbed his and I grabbed mine and off we ran.

We got to the sledding trail and ran along and then dove onto our sleds. We were going downhill, head-first, prone on the sled. Do you remember those kinds of sleds? The ones with the steel runners you would wax and the wooden handles on the side where you could sort of steer? You tied a rope to each handle so you had something to use to pull the sled back up the hill. You made sure you dove onto the rope so it was between you and the sled, and not dragging under the runners. Remember sledding like that?

Well, as usual, Ryan was faster than I was and he was sliding down about ten yards in front of me. It was dusk and I could just see Ryan's form as a black silhouette against the white snow and ice of the trail.

We got going very fast, and as we were nearing the bottom of that sledding hill, we learned that there were jump levels and mounds in the snow. The first level we hit was a jump and suddenly the sled was off the ground.

Wham. The sled and I hit that trail and sped toward the next level which was another jump. I saw Ryan ahead of me as his sled took off and I knew there was nothing I could do but ride it out. After all, how many jumps could there be?

Wham. I landed again and kept on the sled but saw that Ryan was heading over the next jump.

The snow trail was like a washboard and I cannot tell you how many times that ride was 'jump, wham, slide, jump'. Over and over it happened until the sled's momentum was all spent and we slid to a stop just before reaching the frozen lake.

Ryan thought it was great! I was not so sure. A fast pounding, in a dusky twilight, sliding into the unknown was not my idea of fun. I sat out most of the rest of that sledding adventure evening, until Jim, the youth leader convinced me to go down that same trail with him. This time he and I sat on the sled, and we did not run at the start. The jumps at the bottom of the hill were still pretty intense, but not nearly as scary and as ominous when I had a man holding me from behind and the jumps were just hills.

Ups and downs at church. How fitting that is. Jim was like Mrs. K. He helped me in my fears and pains. Is that how Christian should be?

How has your experience at church been? Have you ever been hurt by church people? That is a special kind of pain.

Oh God. It hurts!

6 CHURCH PEOPLE PAIN

As I have said, my sister is six years older than me. At least she was while she was alive. Now that no longer matters so much. That six year period did have a huge significance in our understanding and memories of childhood.

For me, I do not recall our family ever really being a church going family. We did attend rarely, maybe a Christmas or Easter service, but not very often at all. For me, my childhood church experiences were with Mrs. K's family, not with my own.

But my sister remembers her experiences differently. For when I was just a little guy, under four years old or so, our family were members of the neighborhood church. My dad, mom and especially my sister Kay shared their experiences about being part of the church when I was an adult.

My dad would only say, "Yes, we went to *that* church for a while." He really emphasized the word, 'that' like it was a curse word. No mincing involved. He did not elaborate on why they quit going when I was little.

My inquisitive nature and pestering questions finally got an answer on why they quit attending. But let me share with you my sister's experience there before I tell you what happened to my dad.

My sister was a kid about ten years old, in roughly 1963 and the church was making a big push for kids to be in a Junior Choir. My sister got excited and she approached Mrs. G the Reverend's wife.

Kay related that she walked up and asked Mrs. G how and when she could be in the Junior Choir. Mrs. G looked at my sister Kay, and said, "Well, I suppose we can let you in. But you will have to stand in the back, we only want the pretty children in front."

Oh God. It hurts!

You see, my sister was always a chubby kid, and as an adult she is, oh, sorry, was large. She also had thin dark hair and brown eyes. Mrs. G then went on to say, "You see, the pretty children are the ones with blond hair and blue eyes. They are like the angels, and we want everyone to see those children. Yes, you may join, but only in the back row."

My sister did not join that Junior Choir.

That experience tainted my sister on the idea of church for her entire life. My sister was married three times, the first man was basically a pot head, the second man was a nice guy with kids from a previous marriage, but my mother basically ruined that relationship between him and Kay. That last man Kay married, well, I at first thought was an answer to prayer. The two of them drove up to my home, about a three hour drive, and wanted me to do the spiritual wedding for them. I was hopeful and for a short while it looked like Kay had found someone who would help her. Sadly, he was revealed as a manipulative and terribly abusive man.

As to spiritual matters, my sister claimed to be a pagan. She told people she was into wiccan beliefs. She loved nature and plants and rocks. I will share more about Kay's journey later on.

I often wonder what would have happened in my sister's life, if Mrs. G, that choir director, had acted in a Christian manner to her? Where is the love of Jesus in telling a ten year old girl she is basically ugly? How different would that little ten year old girl see church if she had been allowed into that Junior Choir and treated with love and respect and honor?

Well, my dad had a similar experience with the Reverend G of that church. My dad was a contractor, builder, and carpenter. I found out from two different sources, each independent of the other, why my dad stopped attending.

One Sunday morning, a man's basement flooded. My dad went out early and worked to help that man in his crisis. After helping him, dad rushed home, and put on some basic clothing with his usual cowboy boots. He thought that after church he would run back to the man's house to make sure the basement was not flooding again.

So my dad, along with his wife, and his daughter and little son went to that neighborhood church. Before the service even began, Reverend G approached my father. He looked at dad's cowboy boots and with his best preaching voice said, "I am sorry Lloyd, but you must leave and return appropriately dressed for church. We are trying to grow this congregation."

My dad's response was, "I will be happy to leave."

He never went back, except for those rare Christmas or Easter services, and he was not at all active in any other church.

Oh God. It hurts!

If you have been keeping notes, you will know by now that I worked as an ICU RN for ten years. That was until I had my hips replaced. That ended my nursing career and steered me into a different path. I have done other things since 1992 when my hips were replaced. Other things besides having my knees replaces, and my wrist rebuilt, a hip prosthesis revised, and a shoulder replaced. As I write this I am scheduled for my other shoulder to be replaced. But more on those issues later. I have been a patient often.

So let me back up a bit. I attended church often with Ryan and his family. One time at that church, not the church where Reverend G lorded over his flock, which by the way was only a couple blocks from where Mrs. K and her family lived. It is interesting, while I consider it, that Mrs. K's family could have easily attended Reverend G's church, considering how close it was to them geographically. But then it was miles and miles away from them spiritually. And not in a good direction. I wonder if Mrs. K knew something about Reverend G, Mrs. G and the other snobs in that church? She was a perceptive lady. Did I tell you how kind she was to me in my hour of need?

Well, I was sitting with Ryan and his family in the pews of their church. The pastor was explaining about how much Jesus loves each of us. He had an alter call. I do not remember if they were playing "Just As I Am" but one way or the other, I was listening. I wanted very badly to go forward. I wanted to answer Jesus' call for me.

I looked at Ryan and he and his older brother were playing with papers in the pews. We were kids, remember? Well, I was too afraid to go forward and I started to cry.

I actually cried right there in that church.

I was never allowed to cry at home. In fact, had I cried at home, I would have been "given a real reason to cry."

But I cried in my pew and no one slapped me. However, I did not go forward. I wonder how different my life would have been if I had done that? Alas, I will never know, but I do understand that in some weird, strange, and still mysterious way, God was working in my life.

Spoiler alert! When I was seventeen, I did meet Jesus and ask him to be my Savior and Lord. March 7, 1977 was an amazing day filled with pain and joy. You see, out of physical pain came my life-changing encounter with Jesus. I will come back to that story of a car wreck, two broken bones, a tract, and a hospital bed, later on so keep reading.

For now, suffice it to say, I was saved, and I became a Christian, but only years after I cried in the pews at Mrs. K's church.

Now back to church people and the pain they can inflict. For the last seventeen years I have worked with people in the spiritual lives. I work part-time at a wonderful church where we really try to respect, honor, and love all the sinners who come to us. For we are all sinners.

But the stories I hear of other churches! Egad! (oops a minced oath) The pain and suffering some church people inflict on others is just downright dreadful to hear.

Oh God. It hurts!

I will share a few stories here now about the pain church people cause. If you know me and the church I attend, you will not be able to recognize these stories, so please do not try to decode who I am speaking about. All the stories are true, but I have camouflaged the people and stories to keep their privacy. People who are traumatized by church goers do not need to be further hurt in any way. So here are the stories, with their disguises.

I was told by a woman, that when she was a teen she got pregnant. I think I will call her Mary, after all Jesus' mom was an unwed teenager too. Mary went to the church leader where she and her family, and the boy she had been having sex with, and his family were members. Mary explained what had happened, including telling the leader who the boy was. That church guy listened to her and she thought she had found an ally to walk with her in the hard journey of single motherhood. Mary went home feeling some measure of relief and hope. It would not last long.

The following Sunday, that same church leader stood in his pulpit and called out Mary by name. Right from the pulpit he scolded her. He made condemning her personally a part of his message. He pointed her out, by name, and told her she needed to stand up immediately and "confess before God and this assembly your sins of fornication."

How would you feel if you were Mary?

That church leader did not say a thing about the boy who was sitting on the other side of the sanctuary. The church leader know that boy's name, and how he was the father of the unborn baby. He knew all about it, but he said not a word about the boy. It was as if young Mary had fornicated all by herself and gotten pregnant all by herself.

Mary and her family left the church during that tirade of abuse. The parting shots of the church leader were words like, "Repent and confess or face the fires of hell!"

Needless to say, that woman "Mary" held some very hard memories of the pain church people can inflict. And church people do it all in the name of God!

Oh God. It hurts!

The next story is about a family who had a loved one die. At the funeral the minister spoke about the deceased and said things like, "Because he did this _____ (fill in the blank) he probably is not in heaven now." Yes indeed, that minister was judging the eternal state of a person's soul on behaviors, some of which happened years before. Yes, that minister was the one who was passing eternal judgment on that person's soul. I do believe that it is God who is judge and only God knows the eternal fate of anyone. So when that minister was calling down damnation on the deceased, was he putting himself above God?

How much pain and suffering did that minister inflict on a grieving family? Did they need to hear a "warning about hell"? Or did they need to hear the good news that Jesus loves us and when Jesus forgives sins he forgives all our sins? 1John 1:9 "If we confess our sins, he who is faithful and just will forgive us our sins and cleanse us from all unrighteousness."

Confess our sins. What does that mean? Is it making a list and publicly reading off the list? Does it mean living a perfect life? Must every sin be enumerated and specifically confessed?

Can anyone confess each and every sin we have ever done? Nope. I am sure I cannot, and I doubt the honesty of anyone who claims to be able to confess each and every one of his or her sins. However, if we ask for forgiveness of our sins, Jesus cleanses them all away. All of them, not just the ones we confess specifically, and not just the ones we repent from. Sins are forgiven not just in the past, but in the present, and in the future. All sins are forgiven when Jesus washes them away.

I have known church people who really inflicted pain on other people about the "need to repent." Yes, there is a need to repent, but can anyone lead a perfect life? Can anyone actually live a sinless life? If salvation and entry into heaven depends on repenting of all sins, then it is all about works, and not about grace. People are saved by grace, and not by works. Right? Check out Titus 3:4-5 "But when the goodness and loving kindness of God our Savior appeared, Jesus saved us, not because of any works of righteousness that we had done, but according to his mercy, through the water of rebirth and renewal by the Holy Spirit."

So for a church person to claim someone must repent of all sins to be saved, that church person is not preaching the Gospel of grace through faith in Jesus. That church person is preaching a works gospel, which is no gospel at all.

As I have said, I have had multiple joint replacements. Way back in 1992, when I was working as an ICU RN, I came down with severe arthritis and had to have both hips replaced. One in May and one in August. It was a hard time. It was a physically painful time. It was an emotionally painful time as I had my wife and three little kids to think about. How would I support them?

But also, there was a church guy who really hurt me. Shall we call him Vince? That is not his real name. Vince and I had been attending a Bible study together. I thought we were friends, and so I shared with him my concerns and my worries about what was happening. Vince's response really hurt me. He basically told me, "John you need to confess whatever secret sin you are harboring so you will be healed." Vince also said things like, "Well whatever you did to bring this down on you needs to be repented from. That starts with confession." Oh Vince, you hurt me so.

Oh God. It hurts!

Now I am sure I have secret sins. Everyone does, if you consider a secret sin something that is not visible to the whole world. However, nothing is hidden from God. No sin is secret from God, and no sin is unforgiven by God when we ask Jesus to forgive us.

There is a troubling passage in Matthew 12:31 "Therefore I tell you, people will be forgiven for every sin and blasphemy, but blasphemy against the Spirit will not be forgiven." Scholars are really divided on what is that "unforgiveable sin" but let me reassure you. If you have asked Jesus to forgive your sins, you are not committing blasphemy against the Spirit. If you love Jesus, that is the core of everything else. Loving Jesus is the main thing, and trying to unravel what is that "unforgiveable sins" is probably not very helpful at all.

My former friend Vince, who told me I needed to confess some secret sin was in the same camp that hurts so many other people. They are church people who beat up others emotionally and spiritually with their agenda and ideas about faith. I have heard from numerous people that some church person in some church said to them, "If you just have enough faith, you will be healed."

Oh God. It hurts!

Blaming a person for an illness or injury or emotional suffering and claiming it is due to a lack of faith is utter nonsense. None of us human beings can measure someone else's faith. Claiming someone is sick because of a lack of faith is a judgmental, abusive, and mean spirited thing to say. It is hurtful and it is wrong. I am sure some people say things like that out of a good heart and just have a very bad application of ideas, but it is better to say nothing than to say things that are hurtful. Blaming a victim is a hurtful and stupid way to act, and shows no love at all.

Remember Job? That strange Old Testament book we have spoken about a bit. The one where up in Heaven God and Satan are discussing Job and God gives Satan permission to murder Job's family, and to physically and emotionally torture Job. Yes, that book. Well Job has some friends who come to sit with him in his suffering. That ministry of presence is a good thing. It is good and right and helpful to be present with people in their pain, suffering, and anguish. The friends do the right thing by coming to visit. In Job 2:13 we read, "They sat with Job on the ground seven days and seven nights, and no one spoke a word to him, for they saw that his suffering was very great." Their visiting and sitting with Job in silence is about the only right thing they do. Because when they open their mouths, they lash Job with pain.

Was the author of Job talking about the pain church people can inflict on others? Were church people inflicting pain on others way back thousands of years ago when Job was written? Yes, I know the word church should only be applied to Christian groups and the Christian faith started with the New Testament, I know.

So let me phrase it a different way. Here is my question. Have religious people been spiritually abusing others for a long time in many and various ways?

Job's friends sure do. They beat poor Job with their words. It reminds me of my former friend Vince. It also reminds me of the big powerful people I grew up under. Why is it that when someone is suffering, people will come along and inflict more pain? Often done in the name of God. Why?

Eliphaz, Bildad, Zophar, and even Elihu all offer rather poor counsel to Job. They accuse him of causing his own pain by lacking faith, or lacking confession of sin, or lacking enough good works. They basically are teaching the idea that God is a vending machine in the sky. Do good deeds, pull the religious lever, and out pops blessings. Fail to do the right things, and curses come raining down on your head. Divine retribution for works. Yuck.

Now there is some truth that what we do may cause us, or other people real pain. Of course that is true. You drop a bowling ball on your foot and you have caused yourself pain. The physical pain will not be any different if it was an accidental dropping of the bowling ball or if you did it to yourself on purpose. Obviously, you drop a bowling ball on someone else's foot you cause that person pain. Along with physical pain will come emotional pain connected to intention and that kind of stuff. But here, I am not talking about the consequences of our actions. I am talking about looking at deeds and actions as a currency to win blessings or curses.

So that moves me to discuss the "Prosperity gospel" and how it is really a source of pain for many people.

Have you heard about those 'faith movement' people who make claims about how to get God to dispense stuff to you? Do they have the keys to the cosmic vending machine of blessings?

Many years ago my sister Kay read the book, "the Prayer of Jabez" which gets its name from 1Chronicles 4:10 "Jabez called on the God of Israel, saying, 'Oh that you would bless me and enlarge my border, and that your hand might be with me, and that you would keep me from hurt and harm!' And God granted what he asked."

She prayed the prayer as suggested in that book. From her reading of the book, she thought she got the formula right. She felt like she really put her heart and soul into that. She told me, "I really tried it that way. I really did."

Well, her health did not get better. She got more sick in the years that followed. She got breast cancer, had to have surgery which never healed correctly, that resulted in a chronic infection which needed to be drained periodically in painful procedures, and she had heart and kidney problems. Oh, and her diabetes did not get healed either.

Her financial status did not get better. She was unable to work, and she lost her house. She was forced to move into an old trailer and be on a waiting list for disability housing.

Her borders were not expanded. They actually constricted and tightened and closed down.

She felt betrayed as none of the things suggested in that book came true. Even though she really prayed ad really tried that formula, it failed her. She turned away from church because yet again a church guy had hurt her. This time a guy writing a book which she honestly believed.

And so my sister called herself a pagan and listened to rocks, and admired trees, and generally saw church people as "lying, hypocritical bastards" who are only in religion for "money and domination of others."

Oh God. It hurts!

My sister Kay called church people "lying, hypocritical bastards." She did not mean those people were children born out of wedlock, that old definition of the word 'bastard' but rather meant that they people were an unpleasant and despicable person. One of Sylvester's friends, Daffy, would have said to them, "you're despicable" while spitting all over. In reality Kay added other words to that description which were not minced oaths. And you know what? My sister is right.

There are many church people who are lying, hypocritical bastards who are only in religion for money and domination of others. I have met them. I have confronted them. I too have been hurt by them. They are not few and far between.

Here is another example. Brock and Becky, not their real names, were not church attenders. They had twin children who were five years old. They were not married.

Brock and Becky went to a church and felt comfortable. Their children got involved in the church. Things went along well for a number of months, and Brock and Becky felt like they and the twins were becoming part of that church family. They had begun doing a lot with other people in the church. After a bit more time of regular attendance, they decided that they wanted the pastor to do a wedding service for them. They approached the pastor. The conversation went something like this.

Brock: "Pastor, Becky and I have bene together now for seven years."

Pastor: "Hey congratulations. When was your anniversary?"

Becky: "We got together in the spring, but, well, Pastor, we never did get married."

Pastor: "You two are not married?"

Brock: "No. But now, after being here, we would like you to do our wedding. Will you do us the honor?"

Pastor: "You two never were married?"

Becky: "That's right, but we want to now. Will you help us?"

Pastor: "First, you Brock must move out. You two are living in sin. You cannot live together for six months. At that point, you may come back to me and I will consider doing premarital counseling for you. But first, Brock you need to move out and stop your sinful lifestyle."

Brock: "I cannot move out. My family needs me. I will not move away from the twins, and besides, we have been together faithfully for the last seven years. I would never consider leaving my family."

Becky: "I would not let him move out. That is a ridiculous demand."

Pastor: "If you refuse to repent, that is your choice. But I will take this up with the elders, and you are not to take communion again until you repent."

Brock and Becky and their children were driven out of that church over the coming weeks, as the pastor spread the word about their sinful lifestyle. How would you describe that pastor?

Oh God. It hurts!

Currently, I am very fortunate to be in a local church where we work hard against those tendencies. We are not perfect at all, but we do try to keep the main thing the main thing.

What do you think the main thing is about church? A better question might be, what should be the main thing in a church?

Is it about politics?

Now there is a painful subject. I will talk more about the pain of politics later, but for now, just be aware that politics is an ugly thing. Politics should not be the main thing in church.

Is control of people the main thing in church?

Unfortunately, in some churches they are out to control people.

For example, consider what happened to a couple I know. They were living together and had a some children together. They were not married, but they were seeking out spiritual things. Shall we call them Wanda and Willie? Those are not their real names, but their story is real.

So Wanda and Willie go to a church with their children. The first church they attend has a pretty building, nice music programs, and is close to their home. Sounds good so far, right?

Well, Wanda and Willie go in and they have no idea about liturgy, style, or how church operates. They sit down in the sanctuary, but they sit down in someone else's seat! Oh dear.

The person who usually sits in that seat, does not welcome some new family to church. The person who usually sits in that seat just sulks over to sit in someone else's seat. So now another person has been uprooted from her domain and she too is upset. A ripple passes all through the sanctuary because Wanda and Willie attended church.

Needless to say, no one came up and welcomed Wanda and Willie. No one offered a kind word. No one approached and asked a question or offered a handshake. Nothing like that happened, but several people glared at them. And even more people talked about Wanda and Willie behind their backs.

During the worship service, Wanda and Willie felt so uncomfortable that they heard very little of what the pastor was saying, and even though the music was beautiful, the atmosphere ruined any enjoyment of that.

Is excluding outsiders and clustering around in an elitist, snooty attitude the main thing in church?

So Wanda and Willie did not go back to that church. They tried another church instead.

The second church Wanda and Willie attended had a preacher who spoke for forty minutes about how the church needed money. There were flow charts with a rising thermometer-like red scale showing the giving toward some campaign. Wanda and Willie had no idea, even after forty minutes of begging, cajoling, and huckstering by the preacher, what the campaign was really even for or about, except that he was demanding their money.

As they walked out one of their children said, "Did we have to pay to be there?"

Wanda and Willie did not go back to that church either.

Is demanding money the main thing in church?

A few months later, Wanda and Willie felt the call to try church again. They picked a third church and went there.

That third church had someone welcome them at the door. He gave them a smile and ushered them in. He helped them to find a seat and gave them a bulletin. Wanda and Willie were hopeful that maybe they were welcome.

But then came the sermon, or message, or talk. The church guy got up and began yelling all about politics. The people in the pews nodded their heads in affirmation as that church guy launched into a political agenda. He sprinkled God's name into the mix once in a while, but most often it was all about how evil the government is and how wicked the elected politicians are, and how "America is headed to hell."

The entire speech was around two issues. The world was in the proverbial hand-basket all because of "abortion and gays."

Yes, the entire message was about those two issues: homosexuals and abortion. That church guy yelled and screamed and swore. He berated the deaths of babies in abortion, but then called for the deaths of homosexuals. "As the Bible demands, and God expects!" His passion was fueled by hatred and violence.

Wanda and Willie looked in horror at their small children who were seated with them. The hate spewing forth from the pulpit was not at all age appropriate for their kids, and the judgmental and mean spirit which permeated the whole building was frightening. Yet, they were sitting there surrounded by people who were nodding their heads and gushing forth praises toward the man who was speaking like he was in a beer hall of the 1930s Germany.

Wanda and Willie got up in the middle of the service, conspicuous to all, and took their children out of that church.

Is hate the main thing in church?

It was many months before Wanda and Willie even thought of looking for a church to check out, but they still had a spiritual hunger.

So they tried another church.

This one had a few people welcome them with friendly and honest greetings. Someone else offered to show them where the children's programs were in the church and explained to them that there was "children's church" during the worship time. Wanda and Willie were grateful for the information, but kept their children with them on that first visit.

The songs were new, but pleasant. There were coloring pages along with the bulletin. Wanda and Willie enjoyed the style that was not overly formal, but respectful. The message was part of a series the pastor had been doing from a Bible book, and the central idea of the text was that Jesus loves people.

They were encouraged and stayed. They did not agree with every point, nor did they make instant friends with each and every person. Yet they began a relationship with that church because it was keeping the main thing, the main thing.

The main thing in every church should be that Jesus loves you.

When the main thing is lost, the church is failing, and people like Wanda and Willie, and my sister Kay, and a multitude of other people, will see the church as a bunch of lying, hypocritical bastards.

I could give you dozens of other examples of how church people have hurt, abused, and been generally evil to people and driven them away from church. Yes there are church people who are lying, hypocritical bastards who are only in religion for money and domination of others. Oh the pain church people have caused.

Oh God. It hurts!

7 FATE OF MY SISTER

Now I have said that my sister claimed she was a pagan, and into wiccan beliefs. That really troubled me. So I will share the last several days of her life with you here.

My sister had many chronic illnesses: diabetes, hypertension, breast cancer which had a lumpectomy which never healed correctly so she had a chronic infection, several heart attacks, and other issues. Kay and I had talked a lot about her health an also a lot about spiritual issues.

My sister was very ill toward the end of her life. I spoke to her three or four times a week. We live, I guess I need to now say, lived, about two-hundred miles apart, so personal visits were not common, but phone calls and facebook and other things online were. For many years we both played Super Poke Pets (SPP) which was an online site where you could build habitats and decorate them and take care of your virtual pet. You could gift items back and forth and basically play together. In some ways it was like a modern version of Colorforms. Since Kay and I did not play together as children, due to my mom's interference and malicious behind-the-scenes manipulation, we need to reconnect and we did that as adults and played SuperPoke Pets and other online fun stuff.

At one point I decided to try my hand at making stuffed animals. Yes, I sewed together toys for my wife, and each of my daughters, and one for my sister. I used a pattern that had options for a teddy bear, a cat, a rabbit, or a dog. Mine all sort of turned out looking like a combination of all those together. But I made them and I was happy about it. I gave one to my sister made from a tight, spotted leopard style print. She was thrilled and she named it Blessings. She had it on the shelf overlooking her bed. On a note she had titled, 'Just in Case' she wrote, "I want John to have my Blessings Bear. He and I are the only ones to ever touch it and it means a lot to me."

And so over the last few years I called my sister a lot. Often those were calls where we shared our memories from childhood, but sometimes it was just routine day to day kinds of stuff. She would tell me about the charity pantry she was getting some food from, especially after her food stamps were cut. She also would share how the other people in the disability complex where she lived tried to survive on the meager money they had. They all had their own small apartments, but it was a hard life.

No nice and comfy assisted living for my disabled sister. Nope. There was no way she could afford anything like that, and believe me, I tried hard to find ways to get her to a facility that would have met her needs. It is really true in the USA the rich have pride, excess of food, and prosperous ease, but the poor get left behind or at best get meager crumbs. (You may want to read Ezekiel 16:49 about the sins of Sodom)

On January 1, 2015 I called my sister. She sounded down and weak. She told me it was tough to just get to the bathroom and back. She had been in the hospital for some heart issues not too long before, and over the last year or so of her life she had decided she did not want any kinds of resuscitation. She clearly made it known to the doctors and everyone else that she was a DNR, do not resuscitate. She even ordered a bracelet which said DNR do not resuscitate on it. On the other side she had my name and phone number engraved as a way to tell the world who to call.

That night I got the call. I had been waiting for several years to get the call, and it came.

An ER nurse called and asked me if I was John Thornton. I saw on caller ID that the call came from area code 402, and I knew the tone and style of that nurse's voice from my own years in ICU. I asked, "Is this about my sister Kay?" and the nurse told me she was in the ER on life-support.

Oh God. It hurts!

I asked "Why is she was on life support when she is a DNR?"

The nurse was kind and nice and professional, but she could tell I was upset. The nurse told me my sister had gone flat-line in the ambulance. Now that is when the electrical activity of the heart stops. Those wavy lines on the heart monitor go flat which indicates the heart has ceased to function. I knew that was bad.

The ER nurse connected me to the doctor. I talked to the hospitalist. A hospitalist is a Medical Doctor, an MD who works for the hospital. Let's call her Dr. C. She explained what had happened and how Kay had already been intubated and was on the ventilator when she arrived at the ER. Dr. C was moving Kay to ICU.

My sister and I had spoken often about this kind of situation. I knew she never wanted to be on machines. I knew she had made her wishes known. I knew she had appointed me as her power of attorney for health care issues. But I did not know the Nebraska law about ambulance calls. In Nebraska when you call 911, it is assumed you want every aggressive treatment done, and the emergency crews are obligated to provide it, even if you have a DNR bracelet. So my sister was taken to the ICU. It was late in the evening, and I thought Kay was in the worst of all situations; not healthy enough to live, and trapped on life-support machines so she could not die. The limbo world between life and death I had seen too often in ICU with other patients. That situation would have been the worst of all outcomes.

Oh God. It hurts!

I got off the phone and talked to my wife, and our youngest daughter and her boyfriend. Together we all prayed that God would reveal himself to Kay and save her soul. I fully expected her to be brain dead, or severely brain damaged. As she is only 61, I thought that since they got her heart started again, that might mean the blood would pump, but the brain would not work. I seriously was considering immediately driving the three hours to Omaha to physically remove the life-support tubes and machines myself. When I had worked in ICU I had done that before on patients when the doctors declared them brain dead, and as Kay's power of attorney, I was determined to see her wishes respected.

I sent out an email to the prayer line of my church so people would be praying for Kay. I then called back and spoke to the ICU RN who was tending to Kay. As one RN to another we both understood where Kay was in regard to her desires. A bit later, Dr. C called me and asked about what further heroic measures I would authorize. I told her a flat and rather rude, 'none' but Dr. C was very considerate of my decision and she said she would abide by it.

Early the next morning I called to speak to the ICU RN again. I knew they were on 12 hour shifts and wanted to catch her before she went off duty. She told me that Kay had been writing notes, and was insisting the ventilator tube be taken out. That nice RN also told me that Kay had not made any urine all night. I knew that was bad, very bad. I thanked that nurse for her help.

I was getting ready to depart for the long drive to see Kay when Dr. C called me. She said she had just extubated Kay. That means Kay was off life support, and that I could even speak to her. Wow was Kay mad! She had only called the ambulance to help with pain control and Kay was furious that she had ended up on life support. With her usual levels of cursing and choices of words she shared with me how much suffering she was enduring.

We talked and I explained what had happened. I knew she was never going to recover. I am thankful I could speak to her. I called back to the hospital and talked to Dr. C about what the next steps were. We got a palliative care specialist involved. Palliative care is a type of medical practice that focuses on providing pain and symptom relief especially for those cases where someone cannot recover. It is an awesome specialty. Let's call this next doctor, Dr. W. Well she asked me point blank, "Why was your sister not already on hospice?" I told her none of the primary care doctors had offered it. Dr. W was surprised, but I explained how my sister did not get along with doctors very well and had been a stubborn and noncompliant patient.

Well, after a long discussion and a host of other phone calls it was decided that my sister could go to hospice. Most home hospice services really want someone to be there with the patient 24/7, but that was impossible for us. So I spoke to Kay about going to a hospice facility. She would never agree to that. She said, "I know you will not throw me under the bus, but you know I want to go home." So I called the doctors again and explained that she was ready to sign out AMA, against medical advice, unless they could set up at home hospice. They agreed to give it a try. I told them I knew she might die alone, and that Kay also knew she might die alone, and that was acceptable to both of us.

Kay went home late that afternoon.

Hospice nurses came in and set up the things she needed. My wife got to speak to Kay again, and so did I, several times.

That Saturday, I again spoke to Kay and she sounded very medicated, and she said she was comfortable. I spoke to the hospice nurse who was helpful. I made more calls to my other daughters and friends.

Kay told me, "You would like that Dr. C. I am comfortable in my bed here, and I have oxygen and am warm and feel safe."

I thought it was the narcotics speaking. I had not heard my sister say anything nice about a doctor very often.

The next morning, my sister's neighbor, another disabled lady phoned me early. Kay had died. I got that call as I was reading Luke 11:18, "I tell you, even though he will not get up and give you the bread because of friendship, yet because of your shameless audacity he will surely get up and give you as much as you need." I usually read the New Revised Standard Version, but that Sunday morning I was preparing for my Sunday School Class and just happened to read in the New International Version. The phrase "shameless audacity" was right where I was reading when I got the call my sister had died.

Oh God. It hurts!

That passage, where the phrase "shameless audacity" appears is in a parable taught by Jesus. That parable is about a man who has an unexpected visitor come to his house late one night. The man wants to be hospitable and serve some food to his visitor, but he does not have any. So the man runs to his friend's house. He pounds on the door and says, "Hey buddy, give me some bread for my unexpected visitor!"

The friend refuses saying, "You go away, I am in bed, and the kids are tucked in, leave me alone!"

But the man keeps pounding and with shameless audacity demands the bread for his visitor. Finally, the friend gets up and give the man the bread just to get him to go away.

So with shameless audacity I asked Jesus to save my sister.

Did God do anything? Would I ever know? Where was God?

Well, I made some more calls, and arranged for the disposition of my sister's body. She and I had talked about that as well, and did the paperwork years in advance. Her body went to the University of Tennessee's Department of Forensic Anthropology for use in their body farm. Look it up! That place is a really cool way to use a body and it naturally decomposes and helps police, the FBI, and others to solve crimes.

I then went to Sunday School and taught the class. I also made more calls, and spoke to the hospice doctor, Dr. W and informed her that Kay had died. I know doctors sometimes do not hear back on the outcomes of patients, and the nurse in me wanted to make a report. After the Sunday School class, my wife and I grabbed lunch and headed for Omaha. On the way down several signs and wonders happened. Those showed me that God's hand was all over that sad, cold, and yet somehow holy day.

We went through Kay's apartment and found the first answers to all the prayers people had been giving for Kay. One thing I made sure to get was her stuffed bear, Blessings.

Yes, there were many books about being pagan, or wiccan, or weird stuff like that. Her wheelchair had a pentagram on its headrest and a bumper sticker that said, "Neighborhood Witch" instead of "Neighborhood Watch." There were also a collection of her rocks, and stuff like that. There was a hand drawn ink work which I had seen before as a child. It was poster sized and I am not sure who did the original work back in the 1960s. It always frightened me, as it depicted a satanic figure. It was just plain creepy. I took it off the wall of her closet, and I walked through the bitter cold to the dumpster and shredded it while I prayed.

But in addition to that stuff, there were more books by Christian authors than I expected. By the marks on them, and turned down corners, the books were well read. There were books by Barbara Johnson, Bill Myers, and Ted Dekker on her shelves near her bed. They gave me hope for my sister's eternity. A study Bible was there as well.

We also found crosses and several plaques on the wall with 'Footprints' and other famous sayings. Some cross jewelry made from cheap things was there too. Those also gave me hope for my sister's eternity.

It was a hard day.

Oh God. It hurts!

On the way home, that frozen and cold night, my wife got a text message. It was from our youngest daughter, the one who had been there with her boyfriend the night Kay had called the ambulance and went flat-line. That text message informed us that her boyfriend of many years had officially proposed to her. They are to be married in the summer.

Wow, how emotions can run a roller coaster ride in a single day.

The next day, Monday, I was still pondering and thinking about all that had happened. The weather had gotten very dangerous with blowing snow, wind and ice. Lots of things were cancelled, and there would have been no way to travel to Omaha that day. In the evening, I was crying about not knowing the fate of my sister's eternity. Not long after my fit of crying, the phone rang.

It was Dr. C the hospitalist. She spoke to me and told me that she and Kay had had a "long spiritual conversation" just before Kay had been discharged. Dr. C also told me Kay was receptive and listened well, which was different from the anger and spite my sister had showed earlier in that same day, to that same doctor.

Amazing.

Now, I have hope for Kay's eternity. I have no way of judging or knowing, but I have hope. I also had a friend listen and talk with me which reminded of an incident in Jesus life. Four guys have a friend who is sick and confined to his mat. They carry the mat to Jesus, but the house is so crowded they cannot get in. So they go up on the roof, and do some vandalism. They dig down through the roof and ceiling and open it up and lower their sick friend on the mat down to Jesus. In Luke 5:20 we read, "When Jesus saw their faith, he said, 'Friend, your sins are forgiven you.'"

Did you catch that? Jesus looks at the faith of the friends, and then turns to the man and says to him that his sins are forgiven.

So what were the effects of the prayers we lifted? I will never know for sure, but I do have hope. However, there are times when the hope is overwhelmed by the sorrow.

Oh God. It hurts!

8 ELECTRICAL PAIN AND ONE PERCENT PER DAY

So we have talked a bit about physical pain. You have read my thoughts on emotional pain. Then you pushed through my condemnation of the pain that mean and hateful church people do. And you have walked with me a bit on the journey of my sister Kay's death.

Well, what can be next?

How about more stories?

Pain and suffering come in so many a various forms, and I have been the one in pain. I have been the one to inflict pain (more on that later) and I have been the one to try to alleviate pain.

So I invite you to please read on. Remember, I have changed the names and disguised the situations so there is no breech of confidentially, but the events are true.

As an ICU RN I saw more pain than most people observe. There was a man, let's call him Joe, and Joe suffered greatly.

I was working in a Surgical Intensive Care Unit, the SICU. It was a five bed unit with four ward beds, and one bed in an isolation room. Most of the patients came into SICU for one or two nights after a major surgery and then moved out to the floors for further recovery. Remember this was the 1980s so things are a bit different now.

Well, we tried not to use the bed in the room because that was reserved for the sickest of the sick patients. The nurses had nicknamed that room, the Doom Room because if a patient went in there, they seldom came out alive. The room would have patients in there for literally weeks at a time while we did everything we could to fight off their illnesses. Most died in that room.

Then along came the patient I will call Joe. Joe came in for surgery on a foot wound that would not heal. The first surgery was to do a simple amputation of his toe. It did not go well. He had major complications and ended up in SICU. He medically crashed several times, and ended up being moved into the Doom Room because of a nasty infection which had set up in his incision line.

Oh God. It hurts!

Joe got more and more infected. So he had surgery after surgery. Each surgery removed more of his foot, then his ankle, and finally his leg. The last surgery was an above the knee amputation done very quickly because Joe's heart was weak and he was extremely ill.

But after weeks, he slowly pulled through and did get better. It took what seemed like forever, but Joe escaped from the Doom Room, but not until he had endured so very much pain, anguish, and suffering. Joe did rehab on the regular med-surg floor and got better and better and stronger and stronger.

Then, when Joe was scheduled to leave the hospital and go home in just a few days, along with his new artificial leg, he got sick. Yes, Joe's fever came back. This time it was not a virus, nor was it a bacterial infection. This time it was a fungal infection. He was rushed back to the SICU, and we tried again. He was not in the Doom Room, but he died anyway.

All that hard work, gone. All the effort and energy and time, gone. Joe still died.

Oh God. It Hurts!

Do you understand why things like that happen?

Was it all some meaningless chasing after the wind?

Is life just a pointless exercise in futility?

In my on life, I have been on both sides of the needle. I have been the RN giving the shots and starting the IVs and I have been the patient getting poked prodded and shocked. I have had numerous joint replacements, but those are not the only medical things to come into my life. I also have a heart rhythm problem which was revealed after my first hip replacement surgery. I have recurrent episodes of Atrial Fibrillation, unaffectionately known as A-fib.

My first incident of A-fib was in 1992, and I thought it was perhaps just one of the flukes that sometimes happen. It came on me in the recovery room after my first hip replacement and I thought I would not see it again. During that incident my heart rate was not only irregular it was fast. Yuck.

However, with some medications, fluids, and pain control, my heart converted back into normal rhythm which is called, sinus. It has nothing to do with your nasal sinuses, but instead is the steady regular beating of your heart.

Well, my heart does not stay regular all the time. In fact, I have had over seven bouts of A-fib, and most of them involved cardioversion. Cardioversion is when the heart is shocked with electricity to knock it into a normal rhythm. Let me tell you, it is not a fun experience.

So I have been the RN to administer the cardioversions and I have also been the patient who received the cardioversion. I have been on both sides of those paddles. In a way, I have been the burner and the burnee.

On one occasion, I was in A-fib and so I went to the hospital again. Unlike some people, I can always tell when I switch into A-fib. It makes me feel really rotten. I am tempted to use a non-minced oath to describe my times in A-fib, but suffice it to say they are really crummy.

Pardon me now, while I ask a few more questions before I continue with my stories.

Why does God allow things like A-fib, and degenerated joints, and breast cancer, and renal failure, and stokes, and a medical encyclopedia of other ailments to cause so much pain and suffering?

Why does God allow evil people to beat children, and emotionally torture little kids, and traumatize innocents?

Is it all Satan running wild? Or has God done a deal with Satan to let us all be like Job? Or does God just not care?

Has the Joker broken out of Arkham Asylum and is running loose yet again?

Or is there more than just this world?

Back to that specific time I was in A-fib. I was getting cardioverted and the doctor ordered me to have sedation. The first time I was cardioverted, the sedation was inadequate and on the third shock I remember it clearly. It is like what I image a sledge hammer hitting your chest is like. Yup, it is pretty intense. So anyway, I was getting another cardioversion and they gave me the sedation, and shocked my heart. It worked. Often on each incident of cardioversion it has taken a couple or three shocks to get my rhythm straightened out. Well, not flat-line, not that straight, but rather back into normal sinus rhythm.

The sedation had knocked me out. I awoke in a very beautiful place. It had vividly colored flowers, and small pools of water. There were trees all around the grove I was in, and that grove was surrounded by a foggy mist. The colors of the flowers were stupendous. The trees were beautiful with green leaves and knobby brown bark. It was more sweet than I can describe.

I was in the Wood Between the Worlds as described by C. S. Lewis in his "Chronicles of Narnia" series. It was a truly beautiful place. I called out and said, "It is foggy here."

The ER nurse replied, "John, you are just waking up."

I then walked through the fog and was back on the procedure bed in the ER. Of course, I had never really left there, except in my mind. It could be a hallucination caused by medications, or by the cardioversion. It could have been a dream as I might have slipped into sleep from the sedation. Or it could have been something else entirely.

For me it was a comfort.

That event was also a key to help me understand pain, suffering, and the 'love' of God. Oh wow, that is the subtitle for this book. Amazing how that worked out.

As you know now, I have had numerous joint replacements. Not only is a joint replacement a major surgery, it is also the end of one kind of pain and the beginning of another kind of pain.

When I had my joints replaced, each time the joint was very sore and painful and ruined before the surgery. Now you might be saying, "Well duh? Of course the joint was ruined before surgery, otherwise why have the joint replacement?" The surgery installed the new joint, and that old deep bone pain was gone. It was replaced by a new and different kind of pain. What I call rehab or incisional pain.

Rehab pain begins right after surgery, and for me that often meant an overall decreased level of pain. Oh, of course after the first few joint replacements I did play some mind games saying to myself stupid things like, "I could have lived with the old knee longer." I really did not do that too much in the last joint replacements.

But I did need to do the rehab and physical therapy.

Physical therapy is a blessing. It truly and really is. However, physical therapy is a really huge amount of hard work. For me, I always see a joint replacement's physical therapy as a process of getting better one percent per day. Yes, only one percent per day. So in 100 days you will feel 100 percent better. What that 100% is will never be back to what it was like to not have a degenerated joint. No way will an artificial joint ever feel as good as a non-diseased joint. But you will feel better.

During physical therapy it is totally acceptable to call out and say how you are feeling.

Oh God. It hurts!

Physical therapy is a lot more than just physical. It is also mental, emotional, and spiritual. If you approach physical therapy as a holistic way to get better, you will do better. No guarantee, but as a general guide, you will proceed better in physical therapy if you have a positive attitude and see it not as "pain and torture" but rather as a way to gain back abilities. You will never be normal again. But you can get to be as good as possible.

This is the complete opposite of how people get to heaven. Grace is not at all like physical therapy, and I will be getting to that point coming up. But next we need to discuss another couple areas where people are in pain and suffering. I have kind of foreshadowed and hinted about them a bit.

People are being hurt and suffering because of politics, and because of end-times prophets.

Oh God. It hurts!

8 POLITICS AND THE HORRORS OF PAIN

I used to be a trustee, or board member, of a nondenominational seminary. I did that as a volunteer for many years, until the personal politics the president of that place was expounding caused me to resign. I just could not agree with his extreme political agenda, since it did not square with the Bible. So I resigned. That was a painful event to see someone put politics over the top of loving others and being compassionate and kind.

Oh God. It hurts!

Disabled people, like my sister, are often abused by the political powers. In the last year or so of my sister's life her meager food stamps (by whatever official name they were given) were cut back. That inhibited her ability to buy quality food and forced her to depend more on charity. Yes, she could have quit smoking, and I encouraged her to do that, but she could not beat that addiction. Did I ask, why is tobacco legal?

Too many church people attack the disabled, sick, and injured using 2 Thessalonians 3:10 "For even when we were with you, we gave you this command: Anyone unwilling to work should not eat." By the way, that passage is used out of context far too often. If you get a chance read up on it.

Not infrequently people yelled at my sister when she was in public. They would call out insults and things like, "Get a job you fat pig" when she was on her scooter trying to get to the grocery store. She was too sick to drive anymore, and if the weather was adequate she would try to get to the store near her apartment. However, people were mean and nasty to her. I personally witnessed it and even more heard her tell me of what people had done to her. People also accused her of "being lazy" or "being a moocher" or of "gaming the system."

All those comments and the multitude more which were inflicted on that sick woman were simply wrong. In my entire life I have known maybe two people who I thought were maybe pretending to be sicker than they really were. And getting back to the Bible passage in question, it says, "unwilling to work" not "unable to work." That is a crucial distinction. That is where politicians are really missing the major issue. There are people who are unable to work. People like my sister. The vast majority of people I know who are on disability are unable to work, not unwilling.

I really get angered by the claims that people on disability are living some kind of luxury lifestyle. Those comments are just ignorant. From the poor food, the lack of money to buy services she could no longer do herself, and the crummy housing situations, my sister's life on disability was marginal at best. Even if she had used the cigarette money she wasted for other things, that would not have bought much. Living in dire poverty is not anyone's dream of a good life. Yet, far too many politicians make ridiculous claims about the disabled and the poor.

Many of those politicians seem more influenced by the novelist and Russian atheist Ayn Rand than they are by the teachings of Jesus Christ. In brief, Ayn Rand taught a warped philosophy that hated Christianity, embraced all kids of selfishness, and was narcissistic. She despised the poor and needy. A solid case is also made, from her own writings, that Ayn Rand modeled her novel's hero off a vicious child murderer, William Edward Hickman. In short, Ayn Rand taught a horrible ungodly philosophy which is antithetical to Christianity, and yet some politicians embrace and laud her agenda and put in place laws that hurt the vulnerable and needy in society. The politicians attack the weak, the poor, and the disabled. They attack those who Jesus spoke about when he said, "Whatever you do to these least of these among you, you do to me." (See Matthew 25:31-45)

Some people also claim that the government should never be helping the poor. They say that is the church's job. Well, the church certainly is called to help the poor and disabled, but the Bible also says government is God's servant (Romans 13:4). The Bible also speaks often about the role of the King (government) and how he should show compassion on the poor (See Psalm 72 and Proverbs 29:14). And the Old Testament Joseph was called into government service as the second in command of Egypt. Joseph oversaw a food collection and distribution programs, all run by the government, and arranged by God (See Genesis chapter 41). Therefore, those who claim the government has no role in helping the poor are biblically wrong.

Oh God. It Hurts.

The next subject where politics is hurting people is about homosexuals. I wondered a lot about sharing anything in this book about that subject. I personally have hurt people by blanket condemnation of them. However, I was wrong by hurting people and causing them pain. I need to repent. I was guilty of ignoring the major issue, and focusing on minor issues and hurting people by doing that.

I will go off a bit on a tangential issue here. Tattoos.

Leviticus 19:28 says, "You shall not make any gashes in your flesh for the dead or tattoo any marks upon you: I am the LORD."

The Bible prohibits tattoos? Really?

Yes, right there in the book of Leviticus, tattoos are condemned. No ifs ands or buts, tattoos are condemned.

My sister had tattoos. I personally really dislike tattoos, and cannot imagine getting a tattoo myself. I did not like hearing about my sister getting tattoos years ago, but it was her choice. My dad had a tattoo on his arm that he got in World War II. He told me he and some buddies got tattoos after a long night of drinking alcohol. He also said, "It was a dumb idea."

My sister was insulted by church goers because of her tattoos. That just piled on more pain and more hurt to a woman who already was bitter and wounded by church people. How well did condemning her tattoos work on showing her Jesus' love?

So does the prohibition about tattoos apply to today? If not, why not?

The Bible also says that eating some kinds of seafood like shrimp or lobster is unclean or even an abomination. (Leviticus 11:9-12 and Deuteronomy 14:9-10) Does that apply to today as well? If not, why not?

Now back to that other issue. For those who are gay, or homosexual, or whatever similar term you chose to use, those people are first and foremost, people. They are people created in God's image. So no matter what terms or phrases you use, and there are many ugly terms which are just insults that are not minced up at all, we must remember that we are all people. All people are people Jesus commands us to love. Yes, love. Jesus commands us to love our neighbors, and our families, and even our enemies. No one is excluded from Jesus' command to love others.

My sister Kay was married three times, and each ended in a divorce. She also had a number of friends who identified themselves as gay. Kay told me about the way those people were treated by church goers and many many times those stories were really tragic due to the church goer's meanness, hostility and violence. That added fuel to the fire set up between church and my sister by previous church people, and made my sister less likely to want to hear about anything churchy.

So my sister at about age ten was told by the church choir director she was too unattractive to be in the front, and she was insulted by church people because she had tattoos, and then her friends were called ugly vicious names by church people, well is it any wonder she had issues with church stuff?

Oh God. It hurts!

So, since I used a story about how Wanda and Willie encountered a church where the leader spewed hatred toward gay people, shall we look to what the Bible actually says and does not say about this issue?

There are about seven passages that come up regarding the issue of homosexuality. This is out of over 30,000 verses in the Bible. The exact total of Bible verses varies somewhat between Protestant, Roman Catholic, and Orthodox canons of the Bible. The canon is not a military piece of artillery. That weapon is spelled cannon. The word with the single 'n' in the middle 'canon' is defined as an approved list of books. But not matter how you count the numbers, or which version of the Bible you use, or which canon you accept, you can see, the verses on this issue are not a major segment or portion of Scripture.

So what does it all mean? It all sort of depends on who you ask, and how you define terms and phrases in the Bible. Remember, scholars are divided widely on this issue. There are devout, Bible believing and confessing Christians who love Jesus on all sides of this issue. In my opinion, none of the Bible passages are as clear for today's Christian as some claim, and none can be dismissed as easily as others claim. Those passages are in Genesis 19, Leviticus 18, Leviticus 20, Romans 1, 1 Corinthians 6, 1 Timothy 1, and the book of Jude (a short little book).

I wrote a long and deep discussion of each of those passages pointing out the literary style, the cultural contexts, and the related interpretation problems with each one. Not a single passage speaks about loving relationships between people of the same gender, but instead are about gang rape, temple prostitution, sex with angels, are truly ambiguous, or are part of the Hebrew purity code which was replaced by Jesus and the New Testament. Now I may get attacked by some like a blue heeler chews on a pork chop, but I just do not see those verses as a main issue.

So I felt like that eight pages or so I wrote did not really get to the issue of the pain, suffering, and problems church people have inflicted on others. So I chopped it out and went back to questions.

Did I tell you I like questions?

Why is sexual stuff the focus and target of so much meanness by so many groups? The Bible gives us long sin lists and the sexual sins are found in the middle of those lists. The sexual stuff is pulled out and exaggerated to the point of hurting and clobbering people. While other sins, right in the same list, like greed, lying, slander, avarice, and others are ignored or even embraced by some church groups. Why is that?

How often have the greedy been expelled from a church?

How often have gossips been publically humiliated by church people?

How many times have people who eat seafood been called abominations?

We must not use the Bible as a club to beat people with, for that will only turn them away from the love we all need. Yet, in far too many places greed (which is called idolatry, see Colossians 3:5) is pretty much ignored or even applauded, while any kind of sexual thing is looked at as the worst of all possible sins. Why?

Remember our friend King David, the man after God's own heart? Well he was a big sexual sinner. Multiple cases of adultery, and multiple wives, and at least one murder trying to cover over his sexual sins. Ouch!

David's son, Ole King Solomon had seven hundred wives and three hundred concubines (sex slaves). Just check out 1 Kings 11:3 and you will see how Solomon was a huge sexual sinner.   He also wrote a pretty erotic book that is in the Bible called "The Song of Solomon." Should we use King David or King Solomon as examples of biblical marriage?

So let us look briefly at sexual sin in general. There are far more verses condemning sinful sex acts by heterosexuals than there are verses which might apply to gay people. So out of the 30,000+ verses in the Bible only some seven short passages might apply to questions about homosexuality. None of those were from Jesus. Yet Jesus directed condemns fornication and adultery. Jesus also spoke a ton of times on the sins of loving money and being greedy and the spiritual dangers of being rich. Jesus made that abundantly clear in Luke 12:15 "Take care! Be on your guard against all kinds of greed; for one's life does not consist in the abundance of possessions."

By the way, Jesus never mentioned homosexuality. So why do some church people focus only on certain kinds of sexual sins?

It is all so confusing, and yet people are getting hurt and suffering because church goers do not keep their eyes on Jesus and focus on his love for us all.

Oh God. It hurts!

The main issue should be love, and very few church people showed it for my sister. The vast majority of so-called Christians who interacted with my sister were horrible to her. From childhood insults, to abusive words, to judgmental and mean spirited hatred, church goers routinely offended my sister.

I have been more fortunate than Kay was. I have known wonderful church people who showed me love and compassion. However, there were churches who refused to even accept my application or resume for a ministry position. They did that solely because I was divorced and remarried years before I ever went to seminary. Yes, some church people really do obsess about sexual stuff. Nonetheless, overall I have found church people loving. But I am a white man with the privilege that comes from that.

Did my sister bring on herself some of that junk from church people?

Not when she was a kid. As an adult she did get "in your face" sometimes with what she called "the holy rollers." But I can understand that. She was hurt, wounded, and fearful of more condemnation.

Yet, God kept sending those rare, loving people, into my sister's life. Those people like Dr. C who spent a long while speaking about spiritual things to my sister just before she was discharged from the hospital that last time she was there.

So I have some more questions. Surprised?

Whose job is it to judge?

I doubt seriously that Mrs. K would have ever uttered insults to my sister. In fact, my sister Kay once said, "Mrs. K was someone who was genuine, and lived her religion." From Kay that was high praise. In my last phone call to Kay she said, "You would like Dr. C." That was so very telling.

What is our job as people who claim to be Christians? Is it to insult, abuse and traumatize children so as adults they are bitter and see church as a group of hypocritical bastards? Is it the job of Christians to look at the outside of people and find every fault and rip them up with mean words? Or is the main thing to love God, love our neighbors, love ourselves, and even love our enemies? Love trumps all other agendas, in my opinion. I believe I have read that somewhere.

One more word on sexual sin. Jesus set the bar extremely high regarding sexual purity.

Consider Jesus' words in Matthew 5:27-28 "You have heard that it was said, 'You shall not commit adultery.' But I say to you that everyone who looks at a woman with lust has already committed adultery with her in his heart."

Do you see how high Jesus' sets the standard? His teaching applies to looking at men or women in lust. So using Jesus' standard we probably are all sexual sinners. If you have ever looked at a man or woman in lust, then you are an adulterer. I know I am a sexual sinner using Jesus standard. I can say I am a serial sexual sinner, in light of Matthew 5:27-28.

Oh God. It Hurts!

Now as if speaking about homosexuality was not bad enough, I will now address the issue of abortion. For Wanda and Willie encountered that church where a person's political position on gays and abortion was the standard used for evaluating who was a real Christian and who was not.

I am against abortion in all but exceptional cases. As an RN I know there are a variety of exceptional cases where abortion is medically indicated. Those are all tragedies. A prime example of that is what is commonly called a 'tubal pregnancy' also known as an ectopic pregnancy. The surgery to save the mom's life in those cases requires an abortion of the baby. It is a terrible tragedy.

There are other cases as well where abortion is medically indicated.

What about the real life case of a nine-year old girl who was raped by her step-father and became pregnant with twins? Her nine-year old body cannot carry the twins and attempting to do so might very well kill her. That is another case where an abortion is medically indicated.

There are many other situations which fall into that same category. Yet, I have been personally attacked by so called 'pro-life" people because I point out that sometimes an abortion is medically required. I have also been personally attacked and my faith has been questioned because I support contraception use to prevent unplanned pregnancies.

Oh God. It hurts!

I support mandatory coverage of contraception and ready access to contraception because I want to reduce the rate of abortions. It really is simple, reduce the number of unplanned pregnancies, and you reduce the rate of abortion.

So I am also very supportive of contraception use, and contraception coverage by insurance companies, because it does reduce abortion rates. Many studies have shown that where better contraception access is in place, unplanned pregnancy rates go down, and abortion rates go down as well. If this was a textbook I would need to put a footnote there. But you can look it up yourself.

You would think pro-life people would support preventing unplanned pregnancies for that would be a win-win situation for everyone. But no. There are virtually no "pro-life organizations" which support contraception coverage by insurance or even support contraception use in general. Additionally condom use reduces the spread of sexually transmitted diseases, some of which can be fatal, so that too is a bonus.

Supporting contraception should be a prolife issue, but instead, I have been maligned, slandered, and insulted because I know abortion is sometime medically required, and because I support reducing abortion rates through contraception access and usage.

Oh, and there is a concerted effort to attack, smear, and spread false information about contraception. Contraception methods do not cause abortions. Contraception prevents pregnancy, it does not cause abortions.

I considered putting a long and well researched section here about the "Sin of Onan." I deleted most of it because it is too long and does not really get to the pain, suffering, and love of God question. So in brief, the "Sin of Onan" is a medieval philosophy, very loosely connected to the man Onan of Genesis chapter 38. The "Sin of Onan" basically says sex is only for procreation and that any wasting of sperm is sinful. The "Sin of Onan" is not really based on the Bible, for the Song of Solomon clearly shows that sexual expression in marriage is for more than making babies and the Genesis chapter 38 passage is fraught with interpretation difficulties. But as I have said, scholars are divided on the issue.

Tragically, the medieval nonsense about the "Sin of Onan" is the root behind much of the crusade against contraception. Let me repeat, as an RN, and as a pastor, contraception methods do not cause abortions.

Why is there so much division and strife caused by the issue of abortion?

Part of it is misogyny. Some people hate women and want to dominate and control them. My sister encountered people like that. She would ask questions, and she was treated in a really shabby way. I would then call that same person, ask the same question, and get treated with respect. This happened with medical things, and housing things, and in a wide variety of situations and issues.

Oh God. It hurts!

Also, and back to women and babies, have you ever wondered why the same people who are screaming and ranting about putting an end to every abortion are often the same ones who are calling for deep cuts or elimination of programs that help women and children? Why is that? Maybe because supporting unwed mothers and providing public assistance to them is seen "welfare" or as another "big government program"? Or is the real etiology back to the Ayn Rand agenda of attacking the needy and abusing the poor, sick, and disabled?

A prolife person would want to support programs that help women and children. James 1:27 "Religion that is pure and undefiled before God, the Father, is this: to care for orphans and widows in their distress, and to keep oneself unstained by the world."

Some prolife people make the claim, "God is prolife." Have you seen that?

Well here are some of my pesky questions again.

If God is prolife, then why did God order the killing of infants by his followers?

Yup. God did that. In 1 Samuel 15:1-3 "Samuel said to Saul, 'The LORD sent me to anoint you king over his people Israel; now therefore listen to the words of the LORD. Thus says the LORD of hosts, 'I will punish the Amalekites for what they did in opposing the Israelites when they came up out of Egypt. Now go and attack Amalek, and utterly destroy all that they have; do not spare them, but kill both man and woman, child and INFANT, ox and sheep, camel and donkey.'"

I do not have an answer for that. God orders the slaughter of other people groups in the Old Testament as well. It is disturbing. The genocide of entire peoples that was ordered by God, especially the killing of babies is a tough one for me to comprehend. If you want to read more on that topic, and excellent book is: "Show Them No Mercy: 4 Views on God and Canaanite Genocide" which is written by four good scholars. Not surprising, they are divided on the issue of why God ordered the killing of babies, and whole groups of people. Oops! I got dangerously close to needing a footnote and bibliography there, sorry about that.

Also, and back to the abortion topic, there is the very difficult passage in Numbers 5:11-31. I am not sure how to understand this passage, but the passage instructs the priests to do a test on a pregnant woman. She is given a concoction which is called "bitter waters" and these somehow do a test to see if the unborn child was conceived as an act of adultery. If so, then the "bitter waters" causes the woman to lose the unborn baby through an induced miscarriage.

Is God really prolife? Where is God when a woman gets raped? Where is God when a child gets cancer? Where is God when a man get killed in a freak accident leaving a wife and children behind? Just where is God in those really hard and horribly painful times and events and situations?

Oh God. It hurts!

Well, I am all for programs that actually reduce abortion rates.

Shaming women who get pregnant, like the example I wrote about Mary earlier does nothing to reduce abortions. I have heard numerous stories from women who got pregnant and then the church shunned them. Shaming, shunning, and blaming only pushes women away from the church and causes more pain and suffering. Sometimes the shame also pushes women who get pregnant toward abortion clinics.

Story time again. Back when I was in nursing school I had a friend whose older brother got married. Let's call my friend, Sally. Sally was a very religious person from a religious family. Her brother Reggie got married in a big church wedding. Six months later, Reggie and his wife had a baby. A bouncing baby boy that was eight pounds and ten ounces. Sally told me about that and she said, "It is amazing that a premature baby, born three months early, would be so healthy and big."

Who was that family fooling? They were just lying to try to avoid the shame and blame. I can understand the pressures behind what they did. I can be compassionate with the social stigma they were trying to avoid. In a way, they had their own code of silence, except that family had a code of lying. Is that what church people should do?

Sadly, many times the crappy way women are treated, and the shame and blame that is heaped down upon them when they have an unexpected pregnancy, and the cuts in social programs which help women and children, all lead to increased abortion rates.

Oh God. It hurts!

9 PROPHETING OFF PAIN (NOT A TYPO)

Have you ever been afraid?

Well, I have. I once was taken to the All Star Wrestling match (or whatever the official name was) by my dad. It was at the auditorium in Omaha. It was to see "them wrastlers" as my dad called it.

During the match, a real life fist fight broke out in the audience. Someone yelled, "He had brass knuckles" and real fists were flying. Now it was not as bad as my cousins fighting on the driveway after the funeral, but it was a real fight.

My dad picked me up and carried me away down the bleachers. Police whistles blew, and "them wrastlers" stopped their bout and were watching the real fight in the stands as the police broke up a near riot. That was one of the only times I saw my dad look afraid.

Even when he was battling lung cancer he did not look afraid like he did that day when we went to All Star Wresting.

Why do I bring this up here in a book called, "Oh God. It Hurts!" in a chapter that looks like it is a typo?

Well, because I wanted to.

Hey, I answered a question directly. Are you saying, 'It is about time John Thornton did that!' Well, I do have another couple reasons for bringing up All Star Wrestling and my time with my dad.

My dad was a combat veteran from World War II. He was in the US Army Air Corps and he helped build runways on the islands in the Pacific Ocean. He told me, only late in his life, that he had recurring nightmares of Japanese planes flying in over the runway he was working on. The machine gun bullets would spray all over the men doing the building. My dad would turn and run for the fox holes and bunkers they had also built. Forty some years my dad had nightmares about what he endured and saw in war. I sure hope those nightmares ended for my dad when he died in 1989.

Oh God. It hurts!

When my dad came home from World War II he was in for another severe shock. I only learned this story late in my dad's life. He told me about it only briefly, but the pain in his face was immense as he related what happened when he came back from 'fighting the Japs.'

My dad had married before he was shipped overseas. I have no idea what that woman's name was, nor where she was from. I assume it was from the giant metropolitan complex of Loop City, Nebraska: population 1675 in 1940 from one record I found. I am not sure exactly where my dad's first wife came from. It is a mystery. Sort of like where did Cain get his wife?

What my dad said was, "I went off to fight the Japs, and she stayed home and entertained the troops." She had a son, not from my father.

My sister said dad had told her that when he came home, he stopped at a bar in Loop City and had a drink before going out to the dirt farm where his family lived. He was not sure exactly where his wife was, but was going to check in on his family to find out. In the bar he overheard two strangers talking about the "town whore." They had come to Loop City to visit her. My dad realized that they were talking about his wife. How would that be?

Let Johnny come marching home, hurrah!

Well my dad divorced her, and he also kept up his drinking. Remember how Noah got drunk? Well, Proverbs 23:29-33 says "Who has woe? Who has sorrow? Who has strife? Who has complaining? Who has wounds without cause? Who has redness of eyes? Those who linger late over wine, those who keep trying mixed wines. Do not look at wine when it is red, when it sparkles in the cup and goes down smoothly. At the last it bites like a serpent, and stings like an adder. Your eyes will see strange things, and your mind utter perverse things."

Yes, I quoted that passage before.

My dad had woe, and sorrow, and strife, and many reasons to complain. And like Proverbs hints at, my dad turned to alcohol. Like the night he got his tattoo, and the night he found out his first wife had been sleeping around and had a son by another man, my dad turned to alcohol. Far too many times my dad turned to alcohol.

It may have started as a way to self-medicate and shut down the memories of war. Then it probably progressed to drinking just to drink. In the end, it caused great pain and suffering in his life, including a serious car accident, and a bleeding ulcer with a huge surgery.

Oh God. It hurts!

Once when I was a little guy, during the season when my mom would give me bloody noses for most any reason, she came to me one night. I am not sure where my sister Kay was that night. Mom took me with her for a drive. We drove to my dad's office. I remember it was very dark out, and my dad's pickup was at his office. My dad almost always had two cars when I was a kid. He had a work truck, and he had a real estate car. The real estate car was for driving people around from place to place to look at homes or lots. The pickup was for construction type of work.

Well, the pickup was parked at the construction company's office. My dad owned the company, so his being there was not too much of a surprise. What we found when we went inside, was a surprise, at least to me. My dad was drunk and passed out on the floor of his office. His pants were around his ankles, and the lights were all on.

My mom did not slap me during that incident. She just took me back in her car and drove home. On the way I asked, "Why were his pants down?"

For once, no slap for a question. What an odd night! My mom could not really explain it and fumbled over her words. Finally she said, "He tried to get to the bathroom, but did not make it." That answer seemed to make sense to my young mind.

Except for when my sister and I discussed childhood things, there was only one time when I tried to talk to my family about that incident. It sounds kind of like the Noah story, right? Well, at a Thanksgiving dinner a few years later all the big people were sharing stories and laughing at the butts of their jokes. I thought to myself, 'I have a story' and so I started to tell of the time my mom took me to look for my dad.

Her eyes cut into me so violently, that I literally feared for my life. I shut up. My mom covered it over with one of her usual, "John has such an active imagination" comments. Since I was one of the weak, little people, no one paid any more attention to me.

My sister and I spoke at length about my dad and my experience of finding him drunk. My sister, who is six years older than me, told me that dad would sometimes call her to come and get him when he was too drunk to drive home. That was when he would share with her his memories of childhood and his thoughts on life. When I was about fourteen or so, my dad quit drinking. He went cold turkey and just stopped consuming any alcohol. It was about the same time that my sister moved to Texas to live.

My mother, in her typical and wonderful nurturing way, told my sister, "Your dad was able to quit drinking now that you are out of the house."

So I never got the calls from my dad to come and get him when he was drunk. I did get to work with him on many projects and whatnot up until 1979 when his construction company went bankrupt. I went to nursing school, married my first wife, and moved out of state. We had two daughters together and my mom and dad tried hard to be good grandparents to them. My dad stood next to me in the neonatal ICU after my second daughter was born. He had driven up to see her. My oldest daughter called him 'grumpy' because when she was small she could not say 'grandpa' and he liked the nickname.

Mom and dad even offered me some actual support when I got divorced and was a single parent for a couple years to my young daughters. They came to my second wedding in 1988 and there was a time when life was okay. Dad even made a trip up to see my third daughter baptized in June of 1989. He was very sick, but he made it to see his granddaughter.

Then just a couple months later, my dad did make it into the bathroom. He had been sick with the tobacco-caused lung cancer, and he had trouble standing for very long. He had to sit on the toilet just to wash his hands. I phoned him nearly every day, and he tried to be upbeat, but I knew his time was coming. My mom kept working even when my dad was failing in his health. Each day she made him breakfast and would then go to the office. She would come home and check on him at lunch. Well, that day when lunch time came around my mom entered the apartment and found my dad laid out on the floor of the bathroom. His pants were around his ankles, his oxygen tubing was hanging on the door knob, and the water running in the sink.

I came home from taking my daughters to "The Adventures of Milo and Otis" at the theatre. My wife had stayed home with our baby. She had gotten the call about my dad. He died alone, much like my sister.

Oh God. It hurts!

How does this apply to wrestlers in the ring? Or to the title of this chapter?

Well, wrestling is basically a morality play about good guys and bad guys. It is a big entertainment show with heroes and villains and a whole preset and choreographed timeline. They have painful situations, and suffering feuds, and long standing grudges. You can buy tee-shirts, and foam fingers, and magazines listing all the stuff about the drama between the heroes and the villains. You can watch it on TV, or go to some real world convention or bout. It is a show about good and evil.

In the church world, there is another form of big entertainment that is a show about good and evil. You can turn it on and see it on TV, radio, in novels, and in various movies. It is done by the prophets of the end times. It is all a choreographed and scripted act with good guys and bad guys and lots of pain, suffering, and anguish.

Now let me interject, I do believe Jesus will return again. Jesus speaks about that event in Mark 13:32-33 "But about that day or hour no one knows, neither the angels in heaven, nor the Son, but only the Father. Beware, keep alert; for you do not know when the time will come."

So the Bible does not give a timetable for the end-times. Since the day of Pentecost we all have been living in the last days.

But that does not stop the religious charlatans from making a buck off scaring people and being prophets of pain.

Back in high school, I got saved. It was 1977. After getting saved, I started to attend a church where I was first introduced to end-times prophets of pain. But first let me tell you about how pain led me to Jesus.

I was driving a CJ-5 Jeep at that time. I had a friend, shall call her Paula? Well, Paula wanted to drive my jeep, and so I let her. We went around a corner and skidded on some gravel and the jeep rolled over. I broke my leg in two places and when we were hanging there, my leg was twisted in a nasty way.

Paula and the other teen in the jeep were not seriously hurt, and an ambulance came and took me to the hospital. Paula left me a 4 Spiritual Laws booklet. I woke up in the middle of the night and read through that booklet. I prayed and asked Jesus to be my Lord and Savior. I was born again.

I then started to attend Paula's church. Their pastor was a descent and nice man. After my leg healed and the cast was off, I was baptized. My dad and mom came out to see that. My dad looked very pleased.

Then that pastor presented a special series on the End Times. He had gotten materials from a prophet of pain. He had charts and graphs and a big picture of a statue based, he claimed, on the dream of the Babylonian King Nebuchadnezzar, as recorded in the book of Daniel. He had it all lined up and charted out. He taught what is called things like, dispensational, premillennial, pretribulation, and lots of other big words. But remember, scholars are divided on that subject. That pastor never said there were other Christian views or other interpretations. The materials he presented had it all starting with the founding of Israel as a nation in 1948. (That is not an accurate interpretation of the Bible, in my opinion. It was made up by a guy trying to sell his books.)

One of my other friends at that church, let's call her Phyllis, was about my age. She was so convinced that she told me, "John, we never have to worry about going to college or finding someone to marry or anything like that. The rapture will come before we can graduate." Hearing that was kind of scary. It caused pain and suffering. People were wondering who would be left behind and how horrible it would all be. The gruesome details were discussed over and over. The prophet of pain had struck.

I graduated in 1978. Phyllis waited some years after graduation to marry, but she now is married with some children and grandchildren.

You can see these prophets of pain on TV and radio where their dispensational view is promoted. They write bestselling novels with multiple sequels all with graphic and fearful images. The blood, gore, violence, and wrath would be categorized as a horror movie, except these are dubbed as "Christian" as they claim to be based on the Bible.

Over the years I have researched this subject extensively. I have a shelf where I collect books written by some of these kinds of prophets of pain. One is "88 Reasons Why the Rapture Will be in

1988" and many, many more. They all have similar roots which say things like, "Israel was founded in 1948, and a biblical generation is 40 years, so the second coming must happen by 1988." It seems to all hinge on how they see Israel. There are even images of stop-watches and clocks used. Those stop-watches and clocks were apparently all "on hold" for almost 2000 years, but then they started the "final countdown" at Israel's founding in 1948 and we are just counting the minutes until the return.

For example, Harold Egbert Camping set several dates in 2011 and he had billboards which stated, "Jesus Christ will return to Earth on May 21, 2011. The Bible guarantees it."

Harold Camping died in 2013.

And how do the end times prophets of pain get that 1948 date? Here is the Bible verse they use. Mark 13:28 "From the fig tree learn its lesson: as soon as its branch becomes tender and puts forth its leaves, you know that summer is near." See also the similar phrase in Matthew 24:32. Luke 21:29 reads, "Then Jesus told them a parable: "Look at the fig tree and all the trees..." Hum, all the trees? Were all the trees founded in 1948, or does that parable mean something very different?

In the 1960s and early 1970s a man was trying to sell his book, and he invented the idea that Israel is the fig tree in those verses. Of course, Israel is not a literal fig tree, but that was his claim. He sold his book and that idea became popular, even though it has a very dubious and shaky biblical foundation. The fig tree is a fig tree, in the parable it is a symbol for spring coming. It is just not right to connect the nation of Israel and 1948 to the fig tree and even further it is a big leap to connect it all to the end times of the Bible. But as I have said, scholars are divided on that subject.

Did anyone ever collect or make a claim on Harold Camping's guarantee?

All those books on my shelf were false prophets as the dates they set have come and passed. Setting dates for when Jesus would return, or making people feel like they have to study the news and fit every event into some cosmic timeline just causes pain. Those prophets make money off of it with donations, book sales, DVD sales, and other stuff like that. It is a money driven industry. Like vaudeville performers playing for an audience or like "them wrastlers" they put on a good show and make money off of scaring people.

Now again, I do believe the second coming of Jesus will happen, but the prophets of pain are causing lots of people to suffer and be in fear and distress.

Oh God. It hurts!

Now let me explain a bit more about why this is included here. I know several people who got caught up in end-times stuff and gave everything to the end-times hucksters. Those people ended up in poverty because of some religious con-man. Their families suffered so some TV prophet of pain could have more luxury items.

I also know of a man who refuses to make any plans for his own funeral because as he says, "I was born after 1948 so I will live to see the rapture. You can take that to the bank."

How did that work out for my sister? She was born in 1953.

I also think the escapist agenda of those end-times hucksters causes people to focus on dates and charts and nonsense rather than being in service by loving their neighbors. The end-times hucksters also make people believe being proper stewards of the creation does not really matter because, "We will all be raptured away soon and the Earth burned up anyway."

Additionally, the focus on unconditional support of the modern nation of Israel is not biblical. It is political and divisive. Modern Israel is not the biblical Israel. Paul made that abundantly clear in Roman chapter 9 as well as in Galatians 3:28-29 "There is no longer Jew or Greek, there is no longer slave or free, there is no longer male and female; for all of you are one in Christ Jesus. And if you belong to Christ, then you are Abraham's offspring, heirs according to the promise."

Remember, I am not scoffing at the idea that Jesus is coming back. The second coming will happen. I am just offended by the prophets of pain who are bilking money out of people and diverting the attention of Christians away from our call to love others and help take care of the least of these among us.

Oh God. It hurts!

10 PURPOSE OF PAIN

When I have been in atrial fib and had to be cardioverted, that shocking pain was associated with the intent to fix my heart rhythm. I am always sore for a few days after the heart shocking, and from the one incident I remember, I know it was painful.

Joint replacement surgery is painful. It is associated with the attempt to fix the diseased and worn out joint. The rehabilitation afterward is painful and one must suffer through it all. That rehab pain is associated with the goal of restoring as much strength, range of motion, and function to that joint as possible.

Counseling can involve sharing old and painful memories. That emotional pain is associated with trying to cope better with past experiences, building better relationships, and the goal of leading a more healthy and happy life.

Cleaning out my sister's apartment, and doing all the things to get her body shipped to the University of Tennessee's body farm was painful. But I did that with the goal of honoring my sister's final wishes and also with the goal of helping law enforcement and others to solve crimes and to increase scientific knowledge.

In all those situations, I can easily say, oh God, it hurts!

So pain can be associated with positive and good things. We see that explained in one of my wife's favorite Bible passages.

Romans 5:3-5 "And not only that, but we also boast in our sufferings, knowing that suffering produces endurance, and endurance produces character, and character produces hope, and hope does not disappoint us, because God's love has been poured into our hearts through the Holy Spirit that has been given to us."

There are other passages that speak of some kind of positive outcome to pain, trials, suffering, and problems.

James 1:2-4 "My brothers and sisters, whenever you face trials of any kind, consider it nothing but joy, because you know that the testing of your faith produces endurance; and let endurance have its full effect, so that you may be mature and complete, lacking in nothing."

2 Corinthians 4:16-18 "So we do not lose heart. Even though our outer nature is wasting away, our inner nature is being renewed day by day. For this slight momentary affliction is preparing us for an eternal weight of glory beyond all measure, because we look not at what can be seen but at what cannot be seen; for what can be seen is temporary, but what cannot be seen is eternal."

But I cannot not see value in each and every kind of pain or in all manner of suffering. I cannot see how a baby being tortured can bring about anything good. When a young child is killed by a pack of wild dogs, as happened in my home state not long ago, I do not see a redeeming value in it. I cannot fathom why so many evil things occur in the world.

Which, I am afraid to admit, leads me to a verse of the Bible I just do not like very much.

Isaiah 55:8-9 "For my thoughts are not your thoughts, nor are your ways my ways, says the LORD. For as the heavens are higher than the earth, so are my ways higher than your ways and my thoughts than your thoughts."

I really agree with the message in that verse. I truly and honestly do. My pea-sized brain does not compare at all to God's understand and wisdom and knowledge. However, I believe that verse has been used way too often. That verse has been used to stifle discussion and to quell questioning. It is easy to dismiss questions with "Well we cannot understand God's ways." It can be a cop-out to just fall back on that truth and not work and think and ponder what life, the universe and everything is really all about.

Yes, it is true we cannot comprehend all of God's ways, but we should not gloss over the tough issues and things in life we need to wrestle with.

For just like Jacob wrestling with God, I believe we too are called to wrestle with the hard issues in life. We are called to stand up for justice for the oppressed, and to render aid and assistance to others. That is all part of the main thing, loving. Loving God and loving our neighbors and even our enemies.

How hard is it to love your enemy?

Oh God. It hurts!

11 FREE WILL OR PUPPETS? AN ANSWER?

"You have chosen to approach the mysterious dark forest. If you have changed your mind return to page 1. There is a path to your right which looks more like an animal trail than a path a person could walk. There is a tall tree just at the edge of the forest. Its lowest branches are barely within reach. What do you do? If you choose to follow the trail, turn to page…."

Oops! I forgot this is not a choose your own adventure style book.

In this book I have shared with you my personal stories. I have told you about my family members. Did you like meeting my family of origin?

I have also shared with you stories about what people did to my sister and to other people I know.   I have shared with you stories of what people experienced as they sought out the church as a place of comfort, sanctuary, and refuge. Too often they found hateful lying hypocritical bastards who were agenda driven or only wanted money, power, and dominance.

But I have also shared with you stories about people like Ryan, and Mrs. K, and Dr. C and others who kept the main thing, the main thing and actually were a blessing to people. Even people like me and my sister.

So why is there a difference?

In my own life, I have chosen to be a jerk. No not all the time, but far too often I have been a jerk. Yes, there are many times I have just been a mean, angry, jerk. You could ask my first wife about that. My divorce was certainly not all her fault, and I do understand why she left me for someone else. I am glad she found a nice man and together they appear to have had a happy life. I wish them the best.

I have chosen to say things which were painful and hurtful to others. Once when I was an RN another nurse was there and she said, "I have not done anything new and exciting lately."

I replied, "Have you considered suicide?"

Real funny, huh? Not at all. It was a horrible and mean thing to say. Humor that hurts people is not funny. There are so many things like that that I said to others and I would take them back if I could. If you are reading this and I ever offended you, please forgive me. I apologize and I am sorry.

You could ask my patient and understanding wife of over twenty-six years if I was ever a jerk and she would tell you yes. Yet she has helped me to learn a better way. I am forever thankful for that. She is one of the people who are genuinely loving, merciful, and compassionate.

You could ask my children if I have been a jerk to them, and they would tell you yes. I was not a drunk like my father, and I never gave my children a bloody nose like my mom did to me, but I scared them, and said hurtful things, and I know I failed them at times. I think I was better than the people in my family of origin, but that is not saying much at all.

Part of my failures is because of the family of origin I grew up in. Those people were just plain mean; physically, emotionally, and in most every other way. Those big powerful people from my childhood modeled a crappy way of life. They taught me wrong.

Part of my failures with my children was from trying concepts suggested by James Dobson. I know scholars are divided on the issue, but for me his stuff was junk. Dobson's "Strong Willed Child" and "Dare to Discipline" are extremely dangerous books for any person who grew up in an abusive home. James Dobson's writings can be understood, by abuse survivors, as encouraging the domination, manipulation and winning at any cost which the mean people used on me and devastated my own childhood. So just do not read Dobson's books. Try "How Would Jesus Raise a Child?"

written by Teresa Whitehurst instead. That is a much better book as it is more biblically based and respectful toward children.

So do any of those factors excuse any of my behaviors or my words?

No. I am responsible for the things I do and say. There, I gave another clear answer to a question.

I have free will to choose what I do. Certainly the factors in my life have contributed to what I chose to do, or not do, but they never excuse away my choice and my personal responsibility.

So why does God give people choices? Why does God allow people to make evil choices? Why?

Well, that is a tough question. It really is. To start with there is a lot of confusion over the idea that God is all powerful. Omnipotent is the term for that. It does not mean all controlling. God does not control everything like a puppet master on a stage.

Yes, God is the creator.

Yes, God is all powerful. Well, unless you play word games and semantic gymnastics like, "Can God create a rock so big even he cannot lift it?"

Yes, God is all knowing. That is the term omniscient. But does knowing something mean you control it, or just know about it?

Yes, God is present everywhere, well except perhaps for Hell, which is spoken of as separation from God, but that would be a whole other book to discuss all the questions I have about the afterlife. Suffice it to say on this Earth and in the physical creation, God is everywhere. That is called God being omnipresent.

Did you notice that God has a lot of omni words associated with the divine attributes and abilities and characteristics? Unlike the Dodge Omni I had back in the early 1980s, the omni stuff about God is usually describing good things. I really cannot describe my experience with my Dodge Omni as a good thing. It was not really pain and suffering either, but it was a trial. Well, in a way it was a pain. Cars and car repairs are another area where things in life can get messy.

Did God control my decision to buy a used Dodge Omni? Did God control each and every part of that car which broke? Is God all controlling?

If you say yes, then you must agree that God controls the actions of all things. Now that seems okay when you consider the nice stuff like dogs playing fetch, and eagles soaring over your car when you need a sign, and a beautiful sunrise. However, saying God is call controlling also means that God directly controlled me smashing Ryan's hand with a rock, and me moving a hide-a-bed, and God dictated my parents and sister smoking cigarettes. Saying God is all controlling also means God directs serial killers, rapists, terrorists, and every other evil and wicked person. Do you really think God is all controlling?

I do not.

Do human have free-will?

Now I want to avoid the never ending discussion on predestination or free will regarding eternal salvation. That would be yet another book, and a large list of questions. I want to talk here about our life on this planet. Do we have free-will in the choices we make?

A few Bible verses come to mind that affirm we do have free-will in our choices.

John 6:66 "Because of this many of Jesus' disciples turned back and no longer went about with him."

2 Corinthians 9:7 "Each of you must give as you have made up your mind, not reluctantly or under compulsion, for God loves a cheerful giver."

Deuteronomy 30:19 "I call heaven and earth to witness against you today that I have set before you life and death, blessings and curses. Choose life so that you and your descendants may live."

Joshua 24:15 "Now if you are unwilling to serve the LORD, choose this day whom you will serve, whether the gods your ancestors served in the region beyond the River or the gods of the Amorites in whose land you are living; but as for me and my household, we will serve the LORD."

Consider back to the Garden of Eden. Did Adam and Eve have the ability to choose to eat the forbidden fruit or not?

Why give out a rule, if the person is unable to break it? Breaking a rule is a choice, an example of free-will.

Consider our friend Job, in that book where there is a celestial bargain and deal between God and Satan. Satan tortured Job trying to get Job to "curse God." If Job was just a cosmic puppet, then there was no way to pressure Job into deciding.

Ponder our friend Abraham and the command God gave him to sacrifice and murder his own son. Saying sacrifice and murder is kind of redundant for what Abraham was ordered to do. He was commanded to kill his son. Was Abraham given a choice, or was he just a puppet in the hands of an all controlling deity?

Did our friend King David choose to have sex with Bathsheba and then did he choose to murder Uriah? Or was King David a puppet, an automaton, a fleshly robot following its master's programming?

The list could go on and on and on. Think about every bad thing that is described in the Bible, were they choices people made, or were they God being all controlling?

To me, and I could be wrong, I think people have free-will. It think it is part of the main thing, you know, all that stuff about "Love God with all your heart, strength, soul, and mind, and love your neighbors as you love yourself."

Love is the main thing. Love is why God started everything. God created people to be human beings. To be a genuine human being one has to have free-will. To have genuine free-will, there must be good and bad choices. To show genuine love, there must be a choice between loving and not loving. Therefore, God made people with free-will. So with Adam and Eve, God gave them free-will, and to be real free-will there must be both good and bad choices. Hence, the forbidden fruit was required to be there in the garden for the free-will to be legitimate, so that the humans were in fact, real human beings.

Do you see how interconnected free-will is with so many other things?

Genuine love is something that is given, it is a choice, it is a decision. A puppet who is forced by the puppet master to act is incapable of showing genuine love. At best the puppet will put on a good onward show. It might be an impressive performance, like 'them wrastlers' or like the prophets of pain, but if it is all scripted out and all controlled, it is not genuine love. A puppet will never show genuine love, because a puppet cannot make a choice.

A human being is not a puppet. Without free-will, no human could show genuine love. However, there is the flipside to that issue. Human free-will also allows, in fact, it demands, that there will be the possibility of bad decisions. Therefore, free-will requires the potential for pain, suffering, and agony. Free-will is a double edged sword. It can being blessings or curses. Free-will can bring genuine love or vicious hatred. For human beings have the capacity for making decisions for good or for bad. That is the core of free-will.

Human free-will and the bad choices some people make are the origin, the source, of so much pain, suffering, and trouble.

Oh God. It hurts!

12 A THEOLOGICAL ANSWER?

Remember the story I told you about when I was cardioverted and visited the Wood Between the Worlds? That wondrous place described by C. S. Lewis in his "Chronicles of Narnia" series is a truly beautiful place.

I only got to be there because of the suffering I endured and the pain of atrial fib and electric cardioversion. Without that pain and suffering I would not have experienced the Wood Between the Worlds. I did experience it, but I am not sure what kind of experience that was.

So does pain and suffering serve a purpose?

I believe it does, sometimes. Although to be really honest, I cannot fathom a purpose in every incident of pain.

First, pain is a motivator for change. If you put your hand on the hot stove you are motivated to move it away, and quickly.

When my joints got worn out and the pain of walking, or moving was so bad, I was then motivated to make a change. When the pain in my wrist was so bad that I dropped a dish of steaming hot corn as I pulled it from the microwave, I was motivated to change. I would not undergo joint replacement surgery and the weeks of subsequent painful rehab without the motivator of looking to relieve longer term pain. I was motivated because of the goal to reduce pain.

Second, pain is a teacher. If you put your hand on a hot stove, you learn, from the pain, that it hurts to put your hand on the hot stove.

But do we humans learn from pain? Do we respond like we should?

Nope. Too often people keep repeating the same things that lead to pain. Smoking for example is just an exercise in bringing pain into your life over and over and over again. Have I asked, why is tobacco legal?

When I do something stupid, which I have done often, I am reminded of the Bible verse, 2 Peter 2:22 "It has happened to them according to the true proverb, 'The dog turns back to its own vomit,' and, 'The sow is washed only to wallow in the mud'."

Do you like that image? A dog going back it its puke? (No puke is not a King James Version word, but it is more colorful than vomit) Yes, far too often I have not learned from pain and I have repeated things that cause pain to myself, or worse yet, I do and say things that cause pain to others.

Oh God. It hurts!

Third, pain and suffering show us something about our deepest needs. We need help! We need some way to escape the pain and suffering in this world. Not the kind of imagined escape the prophets of pain promote. No, it is not about charts and tables and setting dates for the end of the world. It is not about ignoring the needs of people around you because you know when the end will come. Or you think you do. Those end-times people cause pain, they do not alleviate it. There is no real help in some pie-in-the-sky escapism of being carried away while everyone who you personally dislike is left behind to suffer in agony. Additionally, I am not talking about the false agenda of the prosperity gospel hucksters who promise you riches, fame, and good health if you only send them the money. But of course, those so-called faith guys will just tell you it is your own lack of faith when their promises fail to materialize. You get sick, and they claim it is your lack of faith. You become poor by sending them your money, and they claim your lack of faith led to the poverty. They will never admit their agenda is bogus, and they are causing pain, suffering, and diminishing the witness of the church.

I am speaking about the real escape from pain that comes at the end of our lives, or at the genuine second coming of Jesus Christ. Pain and suffering shows us we need a Savior to lead us away from this world of pain and sorrow.

For no matter how much faith we have, we will still have pain and suffering in our lives. No matter how many good choices we make, we will still have pain and suffering in our lives. No matter how hard we work to improve the lives of others, and we must be doing that, we can never rid the world of all pain and suffering.

Keeping the main thing will help. When we keep love the main thing it will greatly reduce pain and suffering, but on this earth pain and suffering will always exist. We work against it, but it will always be there.

So how do we understand pain, suffering, and the love of God?

Well, let me review a bit more.

I am the last survivor of my family of origin. Those big people were really messed up in many and various ways. They are even buried in different graveyards, probably because of some feud or strife or spite. I can imagine one of them saying something like, "I will not have my body in the same place as those people." Yes, the family I grew up in was warped, twisted, and filled with pain and suffering.

Did you like hearing about mommatroll?

Oh God. It hurts!

I have written a bit about Job here. Now scholars are divided on Job, especially on how to understand that celestial deal-making between God and Satan. One could also argue over the literary style, meaning, and historicity of Job, but that gets off on a tangent which I do not find helpful. For me, and I could be wrong, Job touches me, as a story, about how a guy would perceive the pain and suffering he goes through. Consider, could Job be a parable about life?

Does it ever feel like you are caught in a tug of war between God and Satan?

Does your pain seem to come regardless of what you do? Even

when you are living a righteous and upright life? Your life can be changed in an instant, and you can lose your loved ones, or get stricken with an illness or injury. Yes, life can smack you up the side of your head. Do you wonder why? I bet Job wondered why.

Have you suffered enormous losses like the death of a child? If so, I am sorry for you and I hope you find healing and comfort and better friends than Job had.

For Job's friend were pain inducers in their own ways. They remind me of the prosperity gospel approach. I can easily hear one of them saying, "Well it looks like Job just did not have enough faith." But that would be nonsense.

Job suffers and suffers and is in anguish and pain. He calls out to God and in the end God comes and God says basically, "Were you there?" Job really does not get any answers to his questions. Sort of like most of the questions I have asked in this book. I just do not get answers. The final chapters of Job say that Job got back more than he had lost. That might be okay for material stuff, but what about his kids? Even though Job had other children, it does not say he got back the same kids that were killed by Satan. How can that be fair and right and good and just?

Oh God. It hurts!

David was no stained glass saint. Maybe his story is recorded in the Bible to remind us that we too will make mistakes and will mess things up? David paid dearly for many of his own choices. His family was a mess, and he suffered from the free-will choices he made. In the end, David is remembered as a man after God's own heart, but that might be because he cried out and sought God's help, even when he had messed up greatly.

David looks to have experienced pain and suffering, yet in the end still turns to God. Psalm 13:1-6 "How long, O LORD? Will you forget me forever? How long will you hide your face from me? How long must I bear pain in my soul, and have sorrow in my heart all day long? How long shall my enemy be exalted over me? Consider and answer me, O LORD my God! Give light to my eyes, or I will sleep the sleep of death, and my enemy will say, 'I have prevailed'; my foes will rejoice because I am shaken. But I trusted in your steadfast love; my heart shall rejoice in your salvation. I will sing to the LORD, because he has dealt bountifully with me."

David really messed up and caused lots of people pain and suffering.

Oh God. It hurts!

Noah's story is a warning about drunkenness and family destruction. It is also a story about breaking a code of silence. Noah's drunkenness caused lots of pain and suffering. His ungodly swearing and cursing at his grandson forced Ham and Canaan to run away. That hungover swearing was misunderstood and therefore subsequent generations were inflicted with more pain and suffering. Some church goers even used Noah's drunken cursing to support slavery.

Oh God. It hurts!

In the Old Testament, God ordered the slaughter and genocide and murdering of the infants of various people. I do not get it. I do not see how that pain, suffering, and anguish can serve any positive purpose. When I read about modern day religious zealots and extremists killing people in the name of their religion, I just do not understand it at all.

Oh God. It hurts!

I wrote about Abraham and Isaac a bit. I just do not like the story. I have a hard time understanding how a God of love can call on a father to murder (call it sacrifice as a euphemism if you want), yes murder his child. I know, in the end God intervenes and Isaac is spared. It seems like some grisly and disgusting test the Joker would put a father though. I just do not like it.

Oh God. It hurts!

I do not understand why my sister had to go through all the junk she endured. I do not understand why so many church people were so mean to her so often. I do not understand why God let that happen. I do understand though, that God was still working and bringing good people, real Christian people, into my sister's life all the way to the very end. If my sister had not suffered the intubation, and life-support measures of the ambulance crew she would not have met Dr. C. Without that pain, Kay would not have had times to talk to my wife and to me for the last phone calls. So that final pain, those last couple days makes sense, in a way.

Let me repeat, it looks like God was still reaching out in love to my sister to the very last. Without the pain and suffering my sister Kay went through when the ambulance crew coded her and put her on life support she would not have met Dr. C who had the long spiritual conversation where she was receptive and listened. I also would not have heard Kay say, "You would like Dr. C." That statement from my sister Kay and the context in which she spoke it is profoundly revealing.

So do I have to understand everything?

No.

There I did it again, I gave a direct answer to one of my questions.

The Bible clearly tells us we will not understand it all. In 1 Timothy 3:16 we read, "Without any doubt, the mystery of our religion is great: Jesus was revealed in flesh, vindicated in spirit, seen by angels, proclaimed among Gentiles, believed in throughout the world, taken up in glory."

And that brings us to the main thing. Jesus Christ is the main thing. Loving Jesus is the main thing. Loving others is the main thing. All that love is all tied together around Jesus to make love the main thing.

How much pain and suffering would be reduced if people genuinely loved each other?

And our ability to love Jesus is only because of pain and suffering. I know, that sounds so weird and odd and off-putting. However, I think it is really true. Sure an all-powerful God could have chosen a some other way, but obviously that did not happen. So we are left with Jesus being the main thing. And what is the main thing about Jesus?

Yes, it is about pain and suffering. Love comes to us because of pain and suffering. Not our pain and suffering, but rather the pain and suffering Jesus endured on the cross. The ultimate pain, placed on the ultimate guy, and done for the ultimate reason. The reason was to eventually get rid of all the other pain, suffering, and problems.

Romans 5:8-10 reads, "But God proves his love for us in that while we still were sinners Christ died for us. Much more surely then, now that we have been justified by his blood, will we be saved through him from the wrath of God. For if while we were enemies, we were reconciled to God through the death of his Son, much more surely, having been reconciled, will we be saved by his life."

1 John 4:9-10 reads, "God's love was revealed among us in this way: God sent his only Son into the world so that we might live through him. In this is love, not that we loved God but that he loved us and sent his Son to be the atoning sacrifice for our sins."

Jesus' death on the cross is about pain, suffering, and the love of God.

Again, scholars are divided on the issue, what they call the atonement, but let me share how I see it.

The cross is repulsive in many ways. It was a barbaric, brutal, and bloody way to kill someone. That is repulsive. It was used to not only kill the victim, but to make the victim suffer in pain and agony. The cross was also a political statement. Being hung on a cross was a way to show that Rome had power over the people.

Yes, in many ways, death on a cross is disgusting. It is like Abraham being called to murder Isaac. On a superficial reading of the Bible story, of Jesus dying on the cross, it looks like some kind of perverted divine child abuse.

Oh God. It hurts!

I have been in debates and discussion where people have asked me things like, "If a human father beat his child to a bloody pulp, nailed the body to some boards and displayed it for hours until the kid finally died, would that be love?"

That is an easy question to answer, for me. If a human father did that to his kid, it is a wicked evil crime that should be punished.

However, there are different ways to see the cross. I do not believe it is divine child abuse. I do not believe it was God the Father beating God the Son to death.

Consider the case of a man who sees a group of kids standing on the sidewalk. In the street a car is speeding along right toward them. That man rushes down and throws himself in front of the car, stopping it from hitting all the children. The car crushes that man to death in the process. Is that man a hero?

I think he is. It is the ultimate act of saving love.

The cross is Jesus saving us from pain, suffering, and eternal death. The pain, suffering, and eternal death are a result of people having free-will. In a way, that car speeding along was started and controlled, not by God, but by human free-will.

So if Jesus saved us from pain and suffering by his death on the cross, then why is there still pain and suffering and all those kinds of problems?

In a way I think of it like a joint replacement. Did I tell you I have had lost of those? When Jesus went to the cross he suffered an agonizing death so as to replace what was corrupt and rotten and broken inside of us. Just like an orthopedic surgeon and the team replaces an ground down, pain-filled arthritic joint, with a new one that has working parts and cool, smooth surfaces. So too, when we ask Jesus to save us and forgive our sins, he answers and we are saved. That fixes the problem, the replacement is finished.

Yes, everyone who calls on Jesus is saved. So if my sister called on Jesus he saved her because he loves her and the pain and suffering he did on the cross was for her. Not only that, but he understands all of her history and all of the crummy, rotten, disgusting things that happened to her, and he wants to fix those too. The thief on the cross called on Jesus in the last hours of his life, and Jesus said to him, "Today you will be with me in paradise."

How good is paradise? Far better than the Wood Between the Worlds, I bet!

So in a way, salvation is like the joint replacement surgery. The joint is fixed, but there is still the need for physical therapy. The weeks and months of pain and stretching and exercise and repetition are like what we do in our life. Physical therapy on a diseased and worn out joint usually does nothing but make it more sore. Physical therapy on a new replacement joint helps it to grow stronger and work better.

So too in our lives.

Or think of it this way. When Jesus went to the cross he took all the sin stuff that was ours onto himself. God turned away from Jesus and turned toward us as sin poured into Jesus and was washed off of us. So God looks at us as clean and perfect, because of the pain Jesus suffered.

Jesus exchanged our broken and wore out junk with new stuff.

And again, it comes back to free-will.

Jesus was not forced to go to the cross. Jesus decided to go to the cross. Jesus decided to take that pain and suffering. Therefore, because that pain and suffering was chosen by Jesus, he has freed us from pain and suffering after this life is over.

So where is God in pain and suffering? God is right on the cross enduring the pain and suffering for us. He did that to take away all the pain and suffering, not immediately, but he did to take the pain and suffering away eventually.

In Revelation 7:17 we read, "For the Lamb at the center of the throne will be their shepherd, and he will guide them to springs of the water of life, and God will wipe away every tear from their eyes." And in Revelation 21:4, "Jesus will wipe every tear from their eyes. Death will be no more; mourning and crying and pain will be no more, for the first things have passed away."

So again I ask, where is God when we are in pain? Where is God when we are suffering? Where is God when emotions are flooding us with grief, sorrow, and anguish?

God is there. God is working to get us through this life to where there is no pain, sorrow, or suffering. I wish the pain and suffering would instantly go away, but until our deaths the pain and suffering will continue. But that is not the end of the story.

To prove that Jesus could take away that pain, and suffering, he rose from the dead. Therefore pain, suffering, and all that junk were defeated, so that when we rise in that resurrection after death, we will no longer have any pain or suffering of any kind.

Oh I hope my sister is freed from her suffering and pain and is now in a paradise made for her. Here on earth, she is missed. I am still subject to pain, suffering, and all manner of junk in the fallen world.

In some ways, as I have told people when they have shared their pain and suffering with me, life really sucks. It is just that simple. Life sucks.

Do you ever feel that way?

But just because sometimes like sucks, that is not all there is to it.

What I can also have is hope. Hope for an end to pain. Hope for an end to suffering. Hope for an eternity where Jesus wipes every tear from my eyes, where death and sorrow and pain will be no more.

As to why God does not heal everyone, and take away all the pain and suffering in the present world, well, I just do not know. I have no answer for that. I wish I did. I wish I knew why. But like so many questions in this book, I cannot give a satisfactory answer.

If I had the ability to remove suffering and pain I would do it. Why God choses to not do it now, well, I just do not know. But that brings me back to hope for the future. A bright future after death where pain, and sorrow, and suffering will be no more.

That is my hope for you and for me as well.

So some final questions.

What did you write down on your paper from my question in the introduction?

What? You did not write down your answer? Really? I am terribly and deeply offended. I asked you to get out a paper and write down your answer to the question, "Is the title of this book a prayer or swearing?" I gave you time to do it.

Alas, some of you did not listen. That was an exercise of your free-will, which proves my point that you have free-will.

Hey, if you did do it, bravo! Thank you.

So if you wrote it down or not, my title still needs a definition. "Oh God. It Hurts!" Is that swearing or a prayer? What were your thoughts at the beginning of this book?

What is your answer now?

When the time comes and you cry out, "Oh God. It hurts!" what will those words mean coming from you?

John Thornton

ABOUT THE AUTHOR

I could tell you all about my family of origin, my educational endeavors, my work experiences, and my other adventures in life. I could do that here, but I have chosen not to. It will be much better if you read this book to uncover those facts and come at the issues with preconceived notions about what I will say. For those of you who know me before you read this book, remember these are my opinions and ideas and do not reflect at all on any group, school, or institution I have been associated with in the past. Do not blame anyone for what I write except for me.

Made in the USA
Middletown, DE
23 July 2015